The Adventure of *Supernatural* Discovery

A HANDBOOK ON RECEIVING DIVINE ENCOUNTERS.

Michael Kaylor

ISBN-10: 0615408036
ISBN-13: 9780615408033

Cover design by Michael Kaylor
Cover photo by Shutterstock.com

Published by:

Rivergate Publishing
PO Box 770488
Coral Springs, Fl 33077

RIVER GATE publishing

rivergatepublishing.com

Dedication

I dedicate this book to my wife, Cherrie . "It doesn't matter where you go in life, what you do, or how much you have. It's who you have beside you." Thanks for how you live life. It is an inspiration to me. I love you.

To my children, daughter Stephanie, daughter Tiffany, and son-in-law Lucas Turolla and grand-daughter Isabella Grace, and my son Mike. You are the inspiration for writing this book. May the legacy continue. Just being with you enriches my life beyond words. You are the most treasured gifts that God has entrusted me with.

To my mom and day, Dorthy and James. Without you I would not have the passion for God that I have. Your steadfastness and unending love created in me an unwavering resolve to always walk with God. Thank you from the bottom of my heart.

To my grandfather, Harry Alexander. After a century of life you went home. But your legacy continues. Your eighty years of ministry inspired and encouraged my life. I look forward to the day we are reunited. You are my hero.

Acknowledgements

Randy Clark, thank you for being a friend who released the rivers of God to me while in a dry and thirsty land. It is a joy to journey the kingdom with you.

Robert Barron, thank you for your continual belief in this project. Your steadfast friendship, insight and revelation of life and scriptures are an inspiration. Thank you for all of your suggestions. Your certainly made this a better book.

Bobby and Joyce Covington, you are truly an inspiration to me. Thank you for believing in the destiny on my life. Your kindness goes beyond words and I will forever be grateful.

Ryan Adair, thank you for your unrelenting gift for making sure the "i's" are dotted and the "t's" are crossed. I am grateful beyond words for your ability to edit with inspiration.

Rakel Sampson, thank you for helping me take the first steps in making sense of all of these stories. I love the fact that I can call you my writing professor.

The Gateway Church family, thank you for being steadfast and encouraging and staying the course to see the Kingdom come on the earth. You are the best church family in the world.

What Others Are Saying...

The Adventure of Supernatural Discovery is the inspiring journey of Mike Kaylor's life and ministry. Through an unusual encounter with God in Brazil, he was forever ruined for mere ritual and routine: he had met a supernatural God in a way that made his life "the journey of no return"! Through testimonies and stories of unusual experiences and God's visitations throughout his life, Mike portrays in simplicity and candidness how hungering after God positions us for remaining renewed in God. This book successfully draws the reader into a similar pursuit of the "more" that God offers.

Senior Pastor
of Bethel Church
Redding, California
Author of
When Heaven Invades Earth
and Face to Face with God

I've known Mike Kaylor for many years. He is a man of incredible passion for the deeper things of God. His new book, The Adventure of Supernatural Discovery beautifully portrays the journey of learning to see life from God's perspective rather than our own.

You will quickly realize that what happened to him can happen to you. His captivating experiences make this book hard to put down. The lessons learned from Mike will be invaluable in helping you fulfill the call of God on your life. His extraordinary life stories can help catapult you into your destiny. This magnificent book has given me an intense hunger for more of the supernatural.

Gary Oates
Author of Open My Eyes, Lord
International Conference Speaker

God has sent a book to assist you in your walk in the Spirit. The present day need to elevate people to the walk of the Spirit and the path of the supernatural is so wanted.

Help comes from a God sent book...A must read for all who want more power in their lives with God....

Roberts Liardon
Speaker, Author of God's Generals
Sarasota, Florida

Mike Kaylor is going to take you on a journey. The book you hold is the story of a life committed to God and the astonishing ways the Holy Spirit seized the opportunity. It begins in the hill country of Tennessee and goes to the backwaters of the Amazon. You will visit places you have not seen or knew existed. But earth-travel is not what this book is about. Instead, the journey takes you off the planet and into a dimension which few men are privileged to explore.

I am now in my 60th year of ordained ministry and wish I could have read this book when my pastoral work first began. It would have changed everything.

Mike is an ordinary person like you and me. His only claim to greatness is the God he serves. In response to that gracious attitude, God has been pleased to give him a preview of the promise: "Eye has not seen, nor ear heard, nor have entered into the heart of man the things which God has prepared for those who love Him. But God has revealed them to us through His Spirit. For the Spirit searches all things, yes, the deep things of God" (1 Corinthians 2:9-11). For most of your journey you will leave your suitcase behind. Nor are human eyes and ears the ones with which you will see and hear. Your feet cannot take you there. At God's command, be prepared to step out of your boat and into the "Other Realm." Mike has already been there.

Charles Carrin
Boynton Beach, FL
Conference Speaker and Author
The Edge of Glory–The Powers of the Age to Come

I love reading stories of people's personal encounters with God. It stirs me and reminds me not only how powerful our God is, but how personal He is. Mike's life stories of God capturing His heart for more of Him is an encouraging read. If you need to be stirred and encouraged for more of God's power in your life keep on reading The Adventure of Supernatural Discovery!

Christy Wimber
Senior Pastor & Head Leader
Yorba Linda Vineyard & YLV Resource Center
Yorbalindavineyard.com

I really enjoyed Mike Kaylor's new book - I predict you will too. This is a story about the modern move of God's Spirit in the Church. I don't know about you but I need regular reminders that God is large and in charge. You will get plenty of such encouragement from this book. I hope more books along these lines are on their way."

Steve Sjogren
ServeCoach.com

The Adventure of Supernatural Discovery is filled with hope for the hungry heart. Michael Kaylor's stories of his personal encounters with the Lord are the "deep calling unto deep" - encouraging each of us that there is always more to see, to hear and to experience from the God Who loves us. My wife and I have known Michael and his wife, Cherrie, for more than a decade and we have seen the tangible and powerful fruit of the experiences he describes in Brazil in his life and ministry.

His story can be your story - the same Jesus is ready and willing to overwhelm you with His love, to resurrect your dreams and to clothe you with His power - again. This entire book can be a personal prophesy for you if you will believe it. What God has done, and continues to do, in and through Michael Kaylor - He will do for you if you ask Him. Read this book and, then, ask the Lord Jesus, "Please do it again in my life today."

Robert W. Barron, Esq.
Corporate Attorney
Fort Lauderdale, Florida

Mike Kaylor's book, The Adventure of Supernatural Discovery is an answer to the questions so many believers have when hearing stories of the miraculous from others who are seeing phenomenal moves of the Holy Spirit in their lives.

For those who are tired of not having "their own" stories, this is a book to inspire, encourage, and release you into the destiny that God has for you in the supernatural. The book is rich with everyday God encounters. The hunger that is cultivated for the Presence of God is powerful. As Mike puts it, "Once you taste the presence of the Lord in your life, you will never be satisfied without it." He lives it, as is seen throughout the manuscript as Mike encounters the Lord in many different situations.

The purposeful vision to see the Lord moving in our lives is characterized by a maturity that often allows life's challenges to become life's trials, but that is so that we understand the Lord is building character in us. "It is not the trials that make us strong but what we do in the middle of those trials." Mike and Cherrie are examples of those who demonstrate Jesus in the midst of difficulty. I believe this book will be a great part of the prayer you are praying that God will give you "more than we are asking for!"

Danny Steyne
The Mountain
Columbia, South Carolina

The Adventure of Supernatural Discovery is an invitation to divine encounters as powerful as if you were in a service with Mike Kaylor.

I have attended services with Mike as he told marvelous stories of encounters with God. With each story my hunger and expectation built until I could feel the Holy Spirit like flood waters building behind the dam.

When he began to pray: "God, let Your presence increase, Holy Spirit come, more Lord!" It was like the floodgates of the dam opened. Hearts were filled with the Holy Spirit. The power of God manifested on the hungry and desperate, who had been primed to receive, as they hungered and thirsted for God's presence. Many were healed. Others were burning with heavenly fire.

I pray that as you read this book, your hunger for God's presence will increase. Your heart will become a sacrifice prepared. The fire of God will fall, and you will be consumed by the presence of God.

Bill Johnson says that in the Kingdom of God there is no understanding apart from experience. Mike has a wealth of experience in the Kingdom of God. As you read, feed on his encounters and feast on the eternal realm.

Lee Prock
Pastor, Agape Church
Stephens City, Virginia

Meeting and translating for Mike and Cherrie in Brazil was like coming to a sudden halt at a railroad crossing with lights blinking and big signs staring at us saying, "Stop, Look, Listen"; making us keenly aware that we were at a significant crossroad in our lives and ministry!

What we learned from Mike and the team was that Jesus is the same yesterday, TODAY, and forever, something that we thought we knew and taught, but weren't practicing! I remember vividly teaching the people group we minister to: "Our God is all powerful…" and then seeing a puzzled look on their faces as if to say: "We would like to see that… we see the shamans and witch doctors healing the sick and practicing the supernatural every day!" The Kaylors moved in a spiritual dimension that we knew nothing about. We needed it, we wanted it! We found it! Thank you Mike for sharing your heart so we could!

David and Diana Bailey
Imperatriz, Brazil
Missionaries to The Krikati Tribes

Contents

Foreword

I read Mike Kaylor's book, The Adventure of Supernatural Discovery: A Handbook on Receiving Divine Encounters in one setting during a plane ride. I enjoyed the book and was amazed at some of Mike's experiences. Mike and Cherrie are choice vessels of the Lord, whom I consider personal friends as well as fellow lovers of His presence and advancers of the Kingdom.

I was present when Mike received most of his experiences in Brazil, and I can attest that he has not exaggerated or spoken "evangelistically" about his experiences in Brazil. If anything, he used understatement. How God used him and Cherrie in Imperatriz, Brazil was nothing less than amazing. Cherrie loved them out of cultural blindness to the need for change by shining into the ritual, forms, traditions, and rules, the love of Jesus for the leaders and their people.

This book is a helpful guide to becoming aware of the "more" in God. It creates a hunger for the "more," and builds faith to receive the "more." It is an exciting, moving story of how God has set up divine appointments and experiences with the Holy Spirit to bring Mike and Cherrie into a more intimate, powerful, exciting walk of faith. I believe this book can be used of the Holy Spirit to draw you as well.

This book will open you up if you aren't already aware to other dimensions than this earthly one; dimensions of the Spirit. You will learn from Mike's journey, from his learning, about prophetic dreams and visions, impartations accompanied by electricity, exceeding, uncontainable joy; heavenly heat and fire; divine appointments, healing and how to receive healing; and most important, how to position yourself to enter into these experiences when you find your spiritual life becoming barren.

I encourage you to read The Adventure of Supernatural Discovery and simultaneously be entertained by the story and encouraged that you can enter into such experiences with the Lord.

Randy Clark
Founder of Global Awakening
Author of
There Is More

Preface

There is a place where reality becomes a journey into the unexpected. Where the intangible becomes tangible. Where transformation on the grand scale begins.

How do you explain to someone that an unseen force swept over you and caused you to do things you've never done before? Or that a mist, like water, came over you at the wave of a hand and took you into a realm of physical and spiritual discovery?

And then try to explain that the mere touch of someone laying their hands on you brought open encounters with the reality of the supernatural—experiences which literally bring you to a place in Heaven where God Himself speaks to you with a voice so pure it transforms years of struggle.

These amazing encounters began to happen to me in a country that was far from my home, in a place where the worship of Heaven seemed to dip down and touch the face of Earth. In the town of Londrina, Brazil, I found myself under the weight of the presence of the Lord while being laid out on the floor and being totally overcome by the sound of worship surrounding me. This was the beginning. This was the start of something that would change my life forever.

Upon arriving to my home in the United States I immediately made plans to return to Brazil. I had become consumed with a divine hunger that seemed to be unquenchable as I received more of Him.

I arrived in Curitiba, Brazil and in the basement of a wonderful church my journey continued. Little did I know an encounter that would set the course of my life from that day forward was awaiting me.

What did all of this mean? What has happened since that day? I can honestly say that since the arrival of these encounters in my life, I have seen and been involved in more signs, wonders, healings and other supernatural activity than I had seen or experienced during the entire first thirty years of ministry put together. Not only that, but many times these encounters are imparted or transferred to others when I pray for them.

As John Wimber used to say, "What you now receive, go give it away." I have a new discovered appreciation for that truth!

Introduction

Psalm 119:111 states that "the testimony of the Lord is our inheritance forever" (author's paraphrase from the NKJV).

What God will do for one, He will do for another. He is not a respecter of persons. When we tell the stories of our experience with Him—that story, that testimony is a promise and an invitation to everyone who hears.

We are very familiar with this concept when we give our "testimony" about how we came to Jesus. What we need to realize is that this same "Law of the Kingdom" applies to other experiences with God. If someone else has had an experience with Him—that story is a bridge to your experience with Him.

I was sitting in Harrisburg, Pennsylvania, attending a Global Awakening conference when Bill Johnson began to speak. During his message, he talked about the legacy of the work of God that has been carried down through his family. Bill explained that in order for his children and his children's children to know about the great works of God in his life, he began a journal. It was encouraging to hear that he had several "starts" in developing his journal. I too have many good intentioned journals waiting for me to write more.

Bill's comments struck a chord deep within my heart. It prompted me to follow through with my journaling. One of the greatest joys in my life is being a father. Because of that I wanted my family and those in my family that are yet to come to understand and know that God has placed His hand on our family. And He will never remove it from us.

I have tried journaling in the past with scattered success. But this time it was different. I knew this time that it was being made alive in me by the Holy Spirit. So I began. I began to recount my walk with God making special note of those "strange things" that I could not explain. Looking back I realized that the Lord has divinely encountered me my whole life. I knew the ministry of my father and grandfather, their sermons and songs they had left behind. These stories helped give permanence to my life. I knew that I belonged in this time and place. I wanted my children to know in detail the encounters and the works of the Holy Spirit that had occurred in my life. By reading these stories I wanted them to know that they are not here by chance but by divine providence.

My first thought was if no one else reads what I write except my children and their children then I will be a fulfilled and happy man. The desire of my heart was that it would encourage them to move beyond what was written and expect more in their life than what had happened in mine. In other words, I want to leave a legacy for my family.

While writing about the encounters and testimonies of God in my life, it became evident that God's heart is to encounter us with the revelation of His divine presence. I know that what God will do for one person, He will do for another. So I began to write with the idea of making this journal a training manual, so to speak, on discovering the ongoing touch of a loving Father.

An anointing can be tangibly conveyed. There is the story of Elisha's bones being so filled with anointing that a dead man was brought back to life after his body was thrown into Elisha's grave and came in contact with his bones.[1] Paul's handkerchiefs are another example of how the tangible anointing can be transferred.[2] John G. Lake would have his workers pray over his newsletter before he sent it out. Reports came back to them that as people would pick up the newsletter, some would begin to shake from the presence of God upon the pages.

As I continue to think about the experiences that I have had in my life, I began to wonder if all of us have had unexplainable things happen, but we just ignored them from a lack of understanding of what they were. I know that was the case in my life. At the time there was nowhere to turn for the answers to these encounters in my life.

So I decided to turn the journal into a book with the desire to bring hope into people's lives. It would be a book that would encourage others in the supernatural realms of

---

[1] 2 Kings 13:21
[2] Act 19:12

God. I believe that everyone, deep down inside, desires to know the wonderful experience of passionately encountering Him.

To that end I began to write my journal and the following book is a record of those life-altering encounters as well as simple instructions for positioning ourselves for more.

Chapter 1

Positioning Yourself For More

I pray that the eyes of your heart may be enlightened, so that you will know what is the hope of His calling, what are the riches of the glory of His inheritance in the saints, and what is the surpassing greatness of His power toward us who believe...

—Ephesians 1:18-19

"If discipline is what ultimately drives us in our pursuit of Jesus, eventually we will give up that pursuit. But a man in love, or a woman in love will never quit. I want my life to be characterized by an unrestrained affection for the Son of God."

—Jack Deere

To seek intimacy with God without allowing or having personal encounters may produce a life that is void of passion. Passion is what will lead us to fulfill the desire that is within us. Without it, a Christian's life will become routine and ruled by discipline instead of the fresh breath of the Spirit of life.

Encountering God is a way to understand that as we live in this world we have an unseen connection to an unending source for living that is rooted in an eternal spring of life. It moves us beyond mere theology and into an experiential relationship that energizes our faith in a new dimension. Encounters with God will shape our view of life in the here and now and cause us to live beyond the realm of earthly substance and answers. It awakens the reality of an inheritance that we can walk in now.

In 1 John 5:15,[3] the writer speaks of "knowing" God. The Greek word for "knowing" is defined as "to experience any state or condition" and also "to perceive by any of the senses." This lays forth the truth of the reality of a physical connection and not just an intellectual understanding. To know someone, truly know him or her, I must encounter his or her life face-to-face. I can read about great men and women in history and have an

---

[3] "And if we know that He hears us in whatever we ask, we know that we have the requests which we have asked from Him."

understanding of what they may be like, but if I am to "know" them, I must have personal interaction.

Solomon speaks of the desire of the young Shulamite bride for her lover: "May he kiss me with kisses of his mouth! For your love is better that wine…Draw me after you and let us run together."[4]

That type of involvement is a description of a relationship that is more than a good understanding of a person. How do you think it would go over with my wife if I went to kiss her, and I kissed her with a "thought" instead of an actual touch?

Since Jesus is alive, why shouldn't He be interacting with us in a real, tangible way? Being a father, I cannot imagine being unable to hold or hug my children or look into their eyes to tell them how much I love them. I can write cards and letters to them all day long, but there is no substitution for the face-to-face, heart-to-heart encounter of expressing a father's love.

So why wouldn't He want to encounter us? He does! One of my favorite pictures of this is the story in Luke 15 where the father has been waiting with anticipation and hope for the return of his son. When he sees him, he runs to meet his son and throws his arms around him with great expression and exuberance. The son had no question that he had just encountered his father's love and favor.

You may ask, "If God wants to encounter us then why hasn't He done it for me?" Let me try and help you

[4] Song of Solomon 1:2-4

position yourself for more of Him, for an encounter with Him.

Please understand that there is no formula, no buttons to push or bribes to pay. The issues of the heart are what is front and center with God. My encouragement to you would be to abandon any preset idea of what you can do to get God to meet with you. He desires to meet you more than you know. He isn't withholding Himself as much as we may be missing the point.

Remember the movie City Slickers? Jack Palance, who played the ranch foreman told Billy Crystal's character, Mitch Robbins, that there was only "one thing" that was the secret to life. When I heard that line I couldn't help but think of the story of Mary and Martha in Luke 10. That "one thing" was intimate, passionate relationship with God.

I believe an even better picture of this is found in Matthew 26:6-13.

> "While Jesus was in Bethany in the home of a man known as Simon the Leper, a woman came to him with an alabaster jar of very expensive perfume, which she poured on his head as he was reclining at the table. When the disciples saw this, they were indignant. "Why this waste?" They asked. "This perfume could have been sold at a high price and the money given to the poor." Aware of this Jesus said to them, "Why are you bothering this woman? She has done a

> beautiful thing to me. The poor you will always have with you but you will not always have me. When she poured this perfume on my body, she did it to prepare me for burial. I tell you the truth, wherever this gospel is preached through out the world, what she has done will be told in memory of her."

An "undesirable" woman falls at Jesus' feet and covers them with her perfume, the cost of which was equal to a year's wages. She was abandoned to Him. Nothing was more important to her at that moment than being with Jesus. The pouring out of her heart to Him had such an astounding and eternal impact that Jesus said that wherever the gospel was preached her name would be known. She had a heart which understood that "one thing," true passion and intimacy. Notice that it did not come from something she had learned but from someone she had encountered.

Let us not live in mechanical formality but with honest, unveiled hearts that understand no matter what, my Father has extravagant love for me and He wants to demonstrate it.

I believe the biggest obstacle to encountering our Father is the preconditioned idea that because of our humanity God will keep us at a distance. If there has been one lie which has infected the church and caused a separation of true intimacy and passion it is this lie: "God loves you, but He probably doesn't like you because you're not perfect enough and you have let Him down."

If we are to come boldly before the throne of God, as it says in Hebrews 3:16, how can we if in the back of our minds we are thinking, "I'm sure I've done something God doesn't like. I'm not sure what it is but I'm sure I have. So why would he listen to me and answer my prayers"? We may not be saying this but many are thinking it and living it out in their relationship with God.

The day that I began to fully understand the revelation and "unreligious" truth about the Cross and the Resurrection was the day I began to understand the Scripture, "So if the Son makes you free, you will be free indeed."[5] (author's paraphrase)

Free from sin, yes, but also free from the fear of not measuring up. I was freed from the idea that God was probably upset with me and He was just waiting for a chance to prove it whenever I messed up.

I realized God was in an amazingly great mood and would always be that way toward me. He knew I was not perfect and He was not surprised by my imperfections. In fact, He never expected me to be "good" enough. Jesus did not come to make bad Mike good, but to make dead Mike alive.

The issue was not sin, it was Jesus. The Great Exchange of eternal consequence, the One that was perfect

---

[5] John 8:36

and holy, the One who knew no sin, became sin. It was in order that I, who was not holy or righteous, could exchange my life for His.[6] That's the point. He has given us the gift of righteousness.[7] A gift! Not something that I have to earn (that would be a wage), or something I deserved (that would be a reward given). I stand today before the Father in perfect righteousness because the Righteous One, Jesus, became unrighteous so I could exchange my unrighteousness for His righteousness. It is a gift and I can neither add to it nor take away from it.

I cannot bribe God with my good works to get Him to bless me, love me, or favor me more. If I had to add something to the mix in order to have God love me or smile upon me, then Jesus did not do enough on the cross and His sacrifice was in vain.[8]

But aren't we supposed to be good and do good works? Good works in and of themselves are meaningless if the motive is not right. The Scriptural motive I see for doing good works is so the world will see and glorify the Father in Heaven:

> "Let your light shine before men
> in such a way that they may see
> your good works, and glorify your
> Father who is in heaven" (Matthew 5:16).

---

[6] 2 Corinthians 5:21
[7] Romans 5:17
[8] Galatians 2:15-21

Works, on their own, do not attain God's favor. He is in love with us and it will not change, no matter what you do or don't do. Jesus completed and fulfilled the law. No longer do we live under an obligation to perform good works to attain right standing with God.

St. Augustine said:

> *We must set no good works before faith. Let no man reckon upon his good works before his faith, for where faith was not, good works were not. There is one work in which are all good works, that is faith which worketh by love. If thou hast this, thou hast the ground of all good works.*[9]

You may say, "Yes, but won't people just go out and sin? It's like giving people permission to sin." First of all, people don't need permission to sin. They're doing a great job without it. And secondly, my job is not to manage people's sin. Furthermore, I do not believe that the church's priority should be in the area of sin management. Churches that go around thinking they are in the sin management business will be upset at the message of the gift of righteousness. Why? Because in order to stay in the business of religion they need sin to be front and center. It is their commodity.

Have you ever heard someone say, "He's a good Christian boy," or "She's a good Christian girl"? I think we all know what they mean by that statement, but I've got to ask, at what level of "good" do we attain the status

[9] St. Augustine, The Homilies (1683 ed., 27-28).

of good? Do I need to read two more Scriptures today or pray for five more minutes? Maybe I need to buy groceries for someone or give them a ride somewhere. Where, on the barometer of goodness, do my works cross over to righteousness? I find it interesting that Jesus Himself said there is no one good except the Father.[10] I hope you are hearing my heart here. I do believe in service and honor and doing right. But I believe the proper motive for the action is just as (or more) important than the action itself.

Let's look at this very popular Scripture, but place emphasis on a few different words.

> *But now a righteousness from God, apart from law, has been made known, to which the Law and the Prophets testify. This righteousness from God comes through faith in Jesus Christ to all who believe. There is no difference, for all have sinned and fall short of the glory of God, and are justified freely by his grace through the redemption that came by Christ Jesus. (Romans 3:21-24, NIV).*

If you took any class in church about evangelism I am sure you are very familiar with Romans 3:23. It is used to point out our sin. But I believe the emphasis Paul is trying to make is our new position of righteousness through faith in Christ Jesus! Not that we are sinners—that's a given. We need to hear who we are in Christ and our greatness needs to be pulled out of us. It is hard to produce a life of

[10] Matthew 19:17

great destiny if all you every hear about is our failure to attain perfection. We become what we focus upon and we need to see ourselves through the eyes of the completed work of the cross.

Without spending more time on this, I ask that you go and check it out yourself. We live in the covenant of Grace. Anyone trying to keep one foot in the old while trying to live out of the new may become a schizophrenic Christian.

This brings me back to my point. How can I have abandoned passion and love for someone if I don't trust that they love and accept me unconditionally? I can't. So my understanding about the Cross and Resurrection of Jesus is key to opening my heart for greater experience and encounters with God. When the revelation of His love comes, it's like you have been set free from years of doubt and bondage. It's a life that is based on the overwhelming love of God that keeps transforming me daily through passionate encounters and the ever-flowing grace of His presence. It is His grace that empowers us to be who we are destined to be.

The proper understanding of my position as a friend and a son to my Father is the beginning point to a life of encounters and transformation. Some of the times with Him may be extreme in intensity and others may be as calming as the breath of spring. No matter what form my engagement with the Holy Spirit may take, I know that He is passionately in love with me and all that He has for me and does for me is good. There is nothing in Him except good.

Chapter 2

Is This All There Is?

Those who hunger and
thirst ...will be filled.
— Matthew 5:6 (NIV)

"If I find in myself a desire which no experience in this world can satisfy, the most probable explanation is that I was made for another world."
C.S. Lewis[11]

[11] C.S. Lewis Mere Christianity

To say that I was disillusioned with my life and ministry would be an understatement. Thirty years in ministry and five "movements" later I found myself asking the same question I had asked when I was a teenager in a Baptist church: "Is this all there is?"

I was so desperate for the reality of the presence of God that I found myself consuming books of past revivals and their evangelists. The stories of how God would encounter these men and women caused me to weep over and over asking God, "Where is this in my life?" I would sit with these books in my lap, as tears would fall onto their pages. It was as if God had passed me by.

> *"O God, You are my God; I shall seek You earnestly; my soul thirsts for You, my flesh yearns for You, in a dry and weary land where there is no water"* (Psalm 63:1).

As David wrote this song in the wilderness of Judah, he seemed to capture the essence of what my life had become. What was it that David was longing for? It is answered in verse 2, *"To see Your power and Your glory."* David had experienced the presence of God to a depth that now without it, he felt completely empty. I could relate extremely well to the cry of David's heart.

I felt as if I had awakened from a presumption of Christian life and now found myself contemplating the deep void, or should I say depth of hunger, which was now an all too familiar part my life. I was tired of meeting with God's people but not meeting with God. "If God doesn't show up, I don't want to go on with pretense anymore" was the statement I found myself continually repeating.

It became a struggle to carry on with the everyday responsibilities of being a pastor. As each Sunday approached I would dread the eventual outcome. It seemed like I would leave church with a smile on my face but a heart filled with discouragement. My only solace was the time I would spend in worship always pursuing Him and resting in His presence. Even there I would sometimes feel like He was just beyond my grasp.

I found myself in a place where my future in the ministry seemed destined to be a life no different than that of a person who works at a job and goes through the motions just to survive.

For many years I had known about Randy Clark and crossed paths with him on occasion. I began to hear story after story of the amazing things that were happening on his ministry trips. I knew that no matter what it would take, I had to go. I began to tell others about what I was hearing and of my desire to go on a trip with Randy.

Their comments were: "God can do that here. You don't need to go to Brazil." My response was, "God is not doing it here. He is doing it in Brazil, so I am going to go to Brazil!"

Randy was speaking at a meeting in Toronto several years earlier when my wife had been healed of an un-diagnosable debilitating pain in the upper part of her back and shoulders. The pain was so severe that it left her virtually without the ability to function normally. We were also pastors in the same movement at the time. It was after her healing when I was asked to go on a ministry trip with Randy, I was primed and ready to go.

The stories I had heard told were of tremendous outpourings of power and impartation. I heard of the miracles, signs and wonders that where happening in Randy's ministry trips. If my hunger was to be satisfied, then I needed to go where Heaven seemed to be open. So I made the arrangements and found myself on my first ministry trip with Randy, headed to Brazil.

One of the wonderful blessings of being on the trip was the fact that there was a special time of prayer set aside for impartation to the team. As I stood waiting for "my turn" to be prayed for, my mind raced with excitement and wonder as I saw people respond to prayer with a myriad of reactions. I thought to myself, "What if I am the only one in the room that nothing happens to?" Before I could finish the thought Randy was standing in front of me and was beginning to pray as he laid his hand on my forehead.[12]

---

[12] Deuteronomy 34:9 (NIV): "Now Joshua son of Nun was filled with the spirit of wisdom because Moses had laid his hands on him."
1 Timothy 4:14 (KJV): "Neglect not the gift that is in thee, which was given thee by prophecy, with the laying on of the hands of the presbytery."

I suddenly found myself on my knees with uncontrollable shaking and my arms flailing all over the place. "What is going on?" I thought to myself. Then I realized I was in a place where I could either go with it or try to stop it. Who in their right mind would try and stop the very answer to years of prayer for more of the reality of God? So I said, "Lord, let it come."

What happened next was not what I expected (although to be honest I had no idea what to expect). A heat started on the inside of me until it consumed my whole body from head to toe. I felt like I was on fire! As this impartation continued, I heard the Lord say, "You've wanted it, you've got it!" I felt a strange tingling sensation going into my forehead. My impression was as if an angel was placing his finger in my forehead. This happened three times.

I began to receive an understanding about the realm of the angelic and of the angels that had been assigned to me. I became acutely aware that there were two extremely tall angels standing directly behind me on my left and on my right. What I saw next was a conflict of my own reasoning. I thought, "What was this huge whirlwind type darkness filled with energy and surrounded by angels?"

"Clouds and thick darkness surround Him; Righteousness and justice are the foundation of His throne" (Psalm 97:2).

I needed to give myself permission to accept the reality that was unfolding right before me. At that point all I could do was bow down on my knees.

It was so intense that I was perspiring heavily. As I opened my eyes, I noticed that the floor around me was drenched. I felt like I had been placed in a pool of water due to the perspiration from this fiery encounter.[13]

The next day I was asked to minister at a meeting of two hundred youth which was being held at the same church where we were holding the conference. I was forewarned that these youth were only there because their parents made them come but there were a few who were sincere in their walk with God. As I walked into the room while the band was playing, the Lord spoke very clearly telling me not to preach. After the experience I had with Him earlier I knew what He meant. These kids didn't need another sermon, they needed Him.

When it was time for me to minister I walked up and introduced myself and told them that I was not going to preach to them. Instead we were going to ask for the presence of the Lord to come and minister to us.

At that point I just stepped back and invited the presence of the Lord to come. I waited. It was important not to rush through this or do anything for effect. As we continued to wait I had them stand up and open their hands as if they where going to receive a gift. Within a few minutes the people on the first few rows on the right side of the room began to quietly laugh. Then they started to laugh loudly and began to fall on the floor because they were laughing so hard. I looked over to the left side of the

---

[13] Hebrews 1:7 (NIV): "He makes his angels winds, his servants flames of fire."

room and in the first section there were youth that were beginning to cry. This was an amazing sight to see. But I knew there was more. I had the youth band come back up and begin to worship again.

In the back, a young girl began to jump up and down with great joy and tears in her eyes. The girls around her began to cry also. I asked her to come and tell us what was happening. She told us that she was a ballet dancer all of her life and that she loved to dance. But six months ago she had been in an accident and the ankles in both of her feet where damaged so bad that just to raise up on her toes gave her great pain. She said that as we were standing, something warm came over her and she began to jump up and down on her feet and the pain was gone! She was totally healed!

Then I noticed that a young man had walked into the room. He was looking for someone, but as he took two steps into the room, he fell face first onto the floor. He then began to manifest demons and was taken to another room to be ministered to by two of our team members.

Later when they came back into the room, the young man was completely free and the countenance on his face made him look like a new person.

Another young man came forward and by the look on his face I could tell he was scared. I asked him, "What is wrong?" He replied, "While I was standing there an angel took me and placed me on a table with two arches made of gold up above me. Then" he said, "the angel put his hand into my left side." Nothing like this had ever happened to him before and he was very shaken up. He then asked, "Do you think I am healed?" I asked him what was wrong and he told me that he had diabetes. The angel had placed its hand into his left side, which is where the pancreas is. I told him to go to his doctor and that I believed that something wonderful had happened to him and in him.

This was a pivotal night for me in my expectation of what God wants to do through my life. It was proof that an encounter with God will change the way you live your life from that point on. Although I had seen the power of God move in my meetings before, I had never seen the level of power that was released that night in the meeting. I was beginning to see the fruit from the ministry of impartation.

And if that was not enough, the impartation continued into the next night as others on the ministry team had to carry me out of the meeting because I was unable to stand—much less walk.

From Curitiba we traveled on to a small town named Joinville, on the southeastern coast of Brazil. As the meetings in Joinville began, I found myself sitting on a stage of a very large concrete auditorium that was filled to overflowing with pastors and leaders who had come to listen to an American preacher, Randy Clark, and receive something from God. As Randy was speaking, he began to talk about the fire of God and the testimony of how a tired missionary to China had received a life-altering encounter with God. She was so overcome that for seven days she had to be carried everywhere she went. But the result of that encounter empowered her to take the country of Mozambique for God. Her name is Heidi Baker. He mentioned that a pastor who was with him on this trip had just received a fire baptism[14] in the previous town we had just visited. That pastor was me.

He continued to talk about the fire of God and how the presence of God can overcome an individual so much that they would be incapacitated for hours or even days. It was a divine impartation or transference of power for ministry and transformation.

As he was commenting about the tangible presence of God, he walked over toward me and waved his hand in my direction. As he moved his hand, a presence that I can only describe as a mist, came over me. It was as if I was standing at the bottom of a waterfall and the breeze from the spray of water came in contact with me.

Immediately I began to feel the river of the Holy Spirit flow deep within me—it was like a "bubbling up." The next thing I knew was that I was bent over in the chair, unable to get up. As I tried to sit up straight, I began to rock up and down, but never able to sit up any higher than someone bowing down.

This went on and on until I became very aware that everyone in the room could see me. I wondered at what point this would stop? I knew enough to not stop it because past experiences have taught me that God does not conform to my expectation of encounters.

---

[14] Matthew 3:11

As this encounter continued, my feet began to move as if they where running. So here I am: a reserved pastor, sitting on a stage in front of several thousand other pastors and leaders, rocking back and forth with my feet moving like I am running in place. This went on and on until I fell on the floor. As I tried to make sense of this and stand up, the floor underneath appeared to tilt at a 90-degree angle until I fell on the floor like I was drunk. If that wasn't enough, I began to laugh uncontrollably.

As Jesus said, "Out of your inner most being will flow rivers of living water" (John 7:38, author's paraphrase). Suddenly I had a vision of a large chambered room. An angel had taken me to the entrance and as I looked in, I saw that it was filled with angels scurrying around and distracted. As we stepped into the room, all of the angels flew into a single file as if to receive a military procession. There was a very large number of angels in place and I heard the angel that was with me say, "These are here for you." I was a little startled at that statement. It took me a while to process what I had heard but I soon began to realize that if I was to accomplish all that was in my heart to do, I was going to need a lot of help.[15]

At this point my concern of distracting from Randy's teaching was shoved aside and replaced by an uncontrollable laughter. Charles Finney wrote that after he testified about his experience of being baptized in the

---

[15] Hebrews 1:14 (author's paraphrase): "Are not the angels all ministering spirits (servants) sent out in the service [of God for the assistance] of those who are to inherit salvation?"

Spirit, a usually serious elder of his church "fell into a most spasmodic laughter. It seemed as if it was impossible for him to keep from laughing from the very bottom of his heart."[16]

Randy had called for the ministry team and I thought to myself, "I've got to get up and pray for people." But when I attempted to stand, the floor appeared to turn at a 90-degree angle and I again fell flat on the hard concrete stage. I began to laugh so hard I finally just gave in and laid there.

After a while, I got up on my knees and someone from the crowd climbed up on the stage and hopped on my back as if he wanted me to carry him. I looked around and thought, "What is going on here?" My translator said that he just wanted what I had. Well, he became quite heavy after a while and I rolled him off my back, and as I did I laid on the floor and continued to laugh.

By this time the meeting was over and a couple of guys on the ministry team had to carry me out. They took me to a restaurant that was attached to the building where we were going to have refreshments. They sat me down at a table and I tried not to laugh anymore but I couldn't help myself. I would look at people and just burst out in laughter. I looked around and noticed that there was a table that had chocolate milk on it. I thought, "Oh, I love chocolate milk!" As I began to try to stand up and walk over to the chocolate milk, the floor underneath me appeared to flip at a 90-degree angle once more. Again I

[16] The Autobiography of Charles Finney, Charles Finney

found myself lying on the floor, but this time I was in the middle of a restaurant. I crawled back into my seat and just laid my head down on the table waiting for the bus to arrive. I wanted to get back to my room because I was so exhausted.

In his biography, John G. Lake, states the following:

> *"My soul was crying out to God in a yearning too deep for words, when suddenly it seemed to me, that I had passed under a shower of warm tropical rain, which was not falling upon me, but through me. My spirit, and soul and body under this influence soothed into such a deep still calm, as I had never known. My brain, which had always been so active, became perfectly still. An awe of the presence of God settled over me. I knew it was God.*
>
> *Some moments passed; I do not know how many. The Spirit said, "I have heard your prayers; I have seen your tears. You are now Baptized in the Holy Spirit." Then currents of power began to rush through my being from the crown of my head to the soles of my feet. The shocks of power increased in rapidity, and voltage. As these currents of power would pass through me, they seemed to come upon my head, rush through my body, and through my feet into the floor...My experience has truly been as Jesus said that He*

shall be within you "a well of water, springing up into everlasting life."[17]

As John G. Lake stated, he knew it was God. Though it was something he had never experienced before, the assurance of God's presence as a "warm tropical rain" gave him confidence. That same expression of "rain" seemed to fall on me and through me.

The next day I began to try to process what had happened to me, wondering if it would have any lasting effect on my life. I couldn't find words to express what I was going through but I knew it was very good. That night I did notice a difference during ministry time. As ministry time began, Randy asked me to come and sit with him in a chair on the stage and pray with people as they came through in a line. At first I had flash backs of the early day's of the Oral Roberts crusades that were on television in black and white.

As I began to pray for a young girl, I felt a gust of wind come over me. I looked around thinking a window was open but noticed that the room was totally enclosed. I asked my translator named Rafa if she had felt it and she said no. I just thought, "Oh well," and began to continue to pray. Then it happened again. I knew that it was not my imagination and that something had just swept over me. So I asked Rafa again and she said that she felt nothing but maybe the Lord was making me sensitive to the angelic realm. I then was reminded of what the Lord had shown me concerning the realm of the angelic.

---

[17] John G. Lake – Apostle of Africa pg 16-20

"In speaking of the angels he says, 'He makes his angels winds, his servants flames of fire" (Hebrews 1:7, NIV).

After praying for each one in the very long line, we left to return to the hotel. The sensation of the angelic wind made a deep impression in me. It confirmed the vision of angelic assignment.

The following week I ministered at a Baptist church in another city in Brazil. I was extremely excited. I didn't care if five people showed up or five hundred. I was charged and ready to go. When we got to the church and walked inside, I noticed that it was quite cold. In fact it was cold enough to see your breath when you spoke. The church had no heating but I didn't care. I knew that the fire of God could light the place up.

As I was teaching I noticed a different change in the room's temperature. I began to perspire to the point I took my coat off and it looked as if like I'd just stepped in from the rain. At that point I knew my message was over and I began to call out for people with certain physical conditions to come forward for prayer.

I laid my hand on the forehead of one young man who had come forward for prayer. To my surprise he literally flew back eight feet in the air as I prayed for him. It looked like someone had hauled off and gave him a blow to the jaw. At that point I took a step back and looked at my hand and thought,

"Something is really different."

The next person I prayed for was in need of physical healing. As I began to pray for her, she said that the area of her body where she needed healing was becoming hot. She received the healing fire of the Lord and was totally restored. I moved on to the next person and they told me the same exact thing. Heat was surrounding the area in their body where healing was needed! This was something new for me and my heart became full of gratitude and joy.

I knew then that something wonderful had been imparted to me. I had over thirty years in "full-time" ministry under my belt, but these things had never happened before. One of the exciting things now is that as I pray for impartation for others, many of them seem to receive the same consuming fire of God.[18] As John Wimber[19] once said, "Whatever you receive, go and give it away." I felt like it was Christmas and I was going around giving away free gifts to anyone who would take them.

In Numbers 27:18-23 we see where Moses was commanded to lay his hands on Joshua to "give" him authority. The result of the ministry of impartation can be seen in Deuteronomy 34:9 (NIV) where it says, "Now Joshua son of Nun was filled with the spirit of wisdom because Moses had laid his hands on him."

2 Timothy 1:6 (NIV) gives another example of the impartation of gifts though the laying on of hands.

---

[18] 2 Timothy 1:6

[19] Power Evangelism by John Wimber

"For this reason I remind you to
fan into flame the gift of God,
which is in you through the
laying on of my hands."

There was a tangible spiritual deposit left in the life of Timothy through a transference from the laying on of Paul's hands.

If you are hungry for more in your spiritual walk then I recommend you search out those whom you consider trustworthy and proven and have them lay their hands on you to receive a fresh baptism of His presence. Find those who are operating in the realm that you desire and press in! Become like Jacob who would not give up the fight until he received from the angel the very thing he wanted—a blessing.[20]

[20] Genesis 32:26

Chapter 3

BAM!

About midnight Paul and Silas were praying and singing praises to God...

SUDDENLY...

— Acts 16:25-26

(NIV)

"God will fill the hungry because He Himself has stirred up the hunger. As in the case of prayer, when God prepares the heart to pray, He prepares His ear to hear (Ps. 10: 17). So in the case of spiritual hunger, when God prepares the heart to hunger, He will prepare His hand to fill."

Thomas Watson

Belem is a beautiful city on the northeastern coast of Brazil. We came to this city to be part of a large crusade held at the local soccer stadium. We would also be ministering to several churches in the area.

One of the churches we would visit was a local Foursquare church. The morning of the meeting brought with it a palpable excitement. Everyone seemed to be anticipating a wonderful and powerful service. As the service began I sensed it would be another typical meeting—with the word "typical" meaning no one knew how the meeting would unfold. It would be an adventure.

This church was hungry. They wanted more of God and they were ready to move into whatever God had for them. As it came time for personal ministry, the church was asked if they wanted more. Everyone stood and began to cry out with such volume that the intercessors in the back room came out to see what was happening. It was like a raging river of passion had just been unleashed in the hearts of the people.

My wife, Cherrie, told me later that inside the intercession room they had been pressing in for an outpouring to come to the church now. As they were praying, the intercessors could hear a sound like a roaring wind coming from the sanctuary. It felt like the church was shaking. As Cherrie came into the meeting she saw that the entire church was standing on their feet with hands lifted crying out for more.

She asked Randy what was going on. He explained that he asked them if they wanted the Holy Spirit and suddenly the whole church began to yell out and he "lost" the meeting. With excitement Cherrie replied, The Father and John Wimber are looking down and they are both pleased, "It looks like church to me!" Of course "losing" a meeting in this manner is extremely exciting. The only thing that could be done at this point was to go and lay hands on everyone. There was such a rush to the front of the church that the team had to climb over the pews in order to pray for people.

In the moments that Randy was "losing" the meeting and my wife was interceding, I was sitting up on the stage. As the yelling came forth I suddenly sensed the Holy Spirit began to stir up the "river of living water" deep inside me. I immediately knew what this was and I thought to myself, "Oh no. Here we go again!" The next thing I knew I was on my knees. The fire of God swept over me again and again, causing great drops of sweat to flow off of me. Suddenly I was thrown up and down on the floor as if someone had taken the back of my neck and was pushing me to the floor and raising me back up again. I had to put my hands in front of my forehead to make sure that I didn't get slammed face first into the concrete. Bam! Bam! Bam! This went on and on until my stomach muscles started to cramp up and my neck felt like it was being twisted and turned at a chiropractor's office.

I thought to myself, "Wait a minute. I think there are angels involved here and they are having fun at my expense!"

What happened next was worth any "fun" that the angels wanted to have. I felt a surge that I can only describe as an intense injection of anesthesia and then I was out on the floor.

The next thing I knew was that I was transported in the spirit to a room. There I found myself on my knees with an angel on my left and one on my right. I heard a voice speak to me and as I looked up I knew I was in the presence of the Lord. He said, "I have something that I want to get straight with you. You are my son and I am your Father." It is hard to describe the flood of emotion that came when He spoke those words to me. Those words changed something so deep in me that I would never be the same again.

Jesus said, "The words that I have spoken to you are spirit and are life."[21] I truly understand that the voice of God, one simple statement, can bring a new dimension of life. The core of who you are can be recreated with a freedom and an understanding of sonship and authority that rests only in a foundation of humility and gratitude that only He alone can give.

In a blink of an eye I found myself resting my head on the shoulder of the Lord. It was like a son lying on the chest of his father, resting and being affirmed. The next thing I heard was:

> "As you are going to be in heaven, I want you to be now.[22] All that is in My house is

[21] John 6:63

[22] I John 4:17: "Because as He is, so also are we in this world."

> yours. Why would I want any of my sons and daughters to live any different on earth now than they will when they are with Me? I want their joy complete now, for it will always be complete here. Too many are afraid because they do not understand me as Father. So their joy is not complete. Holiness is joy, but not the 'holiness' of man. Understanding holiness through the work of the Cross releases true Joy."

As the Lord finished speaking I heard a sound or a tone. I am a musician and I had never heard anything like this before. It was the purest, clearest, and most refreshing resonance of tone I had ever heard. Then I understood that it was the sound of Joy. Heaven resounds with the sound of Joy. It is a constant in His presence.

"Splendor and majesty are before Him, strength and joy are in His place" (1 Chronicles 16:27).

I felt frozen in time as I was listening, but then I was suddenly lifted up out of the room. I felt as if I were flying. I saw buildings that seemed to be made of crystal, made with a sense of pureness. After seeing all of this I was brought back to myself.

A couple of hours had passed and the church was empty except for my wife and our friends, Gary and Kathi

---

2 Peter 1:3 (author's paraphrase): "As His divine power has given to us all things that pertain to life and godliness, through the knowledge of Him who called us by glory and virtue."

Oates. They picked me up and helped me walk to a waiting cab. I wasn't able to stand up—much less walk. When we arrived at the hotel, Gary and the bellman carried me to our room where I was able to lie down on the bed. I felt totally wasted and exhausted but I asked Cherrie to get my journal and begin to write down all the things I was about to tell her of what had just happened.

For the next three days a spiritual residue lingered within me. Whenever I spoke about the things of God, a sensation of heat would begin on the inside of my chest and continue until I was done speaking. The heat was so intense that I could feel it rise from under the collar of my shirt.

This encounter is not new. Read the following account from Jonathan Edwards concerning one of his meetings:

> *Many have had their religious affections raised far beyond what they had ever been before; and there were some instances of persons lying in a sort of trance, remaining perhaps for a whole twenty-four hours motionless, and with their senses locked up; but in the mean time under strong imaginations, as though they went to heaven and had there a vision of glorious and delightful objects.*[23]

I had never related holiness and joy together before this encounter. I knew Jesus exchanged His righteousness for my unrighteousness so that I can be called holy, a child of God. But I never imagined a joyous type of holiness.

---

[23] Account of the Revival of Religion in Northampton 1740-1742:

When this word "holiness" is spoken, most people think of something totally opposite of joy. For many it dredges up images of wailing and crying, or perhaps a solemn faced person whose appearance is anything but joy. Later as I thought about this, I realized that to truly understand the complete work of the cross was to find myself, not just positionally, but experientially in complete right standing with God. No matter what I do or don't do, I cannot add to the work of the cross to produce more of God's love and acceptance on my behalf. I knew that I could not, by my good works, twist God's arm into having Him love me more. He is not mad at me or upset with me. He sees my life completely hidden in Christ by faith in the work of the cross and the Resurrection.

This revelation reminded me of an amazing portion of Scripture found in Nehemiah 8:11-12. Nehemiah had just completed rebuilding the wall of Jerusalem. This chapter describes the reading of the law of God for the first time in many years. As the people heard the law being read they began to be grieved and mourn. Nehemiah stood up and said, "Do not be grieved, for the joy of the Lord is your strength…Be still for the day is holy; do not be grieved…All the people went their way to eat, to drink and to celebrate" (author's paraphrase). There it was again—joy and holiness together.

When I allow myself to receive the unconditional love that has been given to me, it releases the joy of being totally loved and accepted. A revelation of the gift of holiness and righteousness allows us to joyously and boldly come before the throne of God.[24] I believe this is a needed experience for today. It is what enabled me to have true faith. I can live with confidence in His favor. I can stop living with uncertainty. I'm not caught up in thinking "I have surely done something somewhere that has upset God so in the end I know He won't answer my prayer."

This flawed understanding must be corrected by a fresh revelation of His love for us through the work of the cross. Jesus paid the penalty for sin for all for us. God will not judge the sin twice. God is not upset with us because of the complete act of divine exchange through the cross and the resurrection of Christ. We are His highly favored sons and daughters, secure in the Father's house where all things are good.

If you have been hungry to experience more of God here you will find a simple prayer that may bring what you are hoping for. God wants to encounter us more than we know. Let your heart be open to what He may give to you during this time of prayer. You may want to put this book down after praying and begin to soak with some worship music. Open your heart to Him—don't be in a rush. Let His presence come upon you. If you begin to feel

---

[24] Romans 5:17 (NIV): "For if, by the trespass of the one man, death reigned through that one man, how much more will those who receive God's abundant provision of grace and of the gift of righteousness reign in life through the one man, Jesus Christ."

1 Corinthians 1:30 (NLT): "God has united you with Christ Jesus. For our benefit God made him to be wisdom itself. Christ made us right with God; he made us pure and holy, and he freed us from sin."

something happen, I encourage you to go with it. Don't let your mind stop what God may have for you. I want to first pray for you and then I want you to ask God for more of Him.

"Father, I want to thank You that with You there is always more. Your presence is beyond what we can think or imagine. I want to thank You for Your faithfulness in meeting with us and releasing Your fire—Your presence—to us. I am asking that You release an impartation of Your joy and living fire now that goes beyond what is being asked for. I ask You Father, for more! More of Your fire! Come Holy Spirit. Increase Your fire upon us now. Overwhelm us with Your amazing love and give to us more than what we are asking for."

Now, it is important for you to ask the Father for what you want.

"Father, I am asking for the fire of Your presence. I am asking that right here, as we are together, that You release to me a fresh baptism of fire and joy. I receive the fire of Your presence. I receive the breath of Your Spirit. Increase in me Your presence Holy Spirit. Increase Your fire within me. Increase Your joy. I am hungry for more. Come, fire of God. Come now upon me. Drench me in Your love Father. Overwhelm me with Your presence. Fill me afresh! Fill me now! I am so in love with You and I long for Your embrace. I want and need to know that I am Yours. Father, let Your presence come."

Chapter 4

When Love Came To Town

In every place that the river goes, there is life.
— Ezekiel 47:9
(author's paraphrase)

"In the evening of life, we will be judged on love alone."
St. John of the Cross[25]

[25] Christian Mystic and Poet (1542-1591)

My wife Cherrie and I flew into the city of Imperatriz, Brazil, for a ministry trip that would last over a month. The main group we were ministering to was made up of 108 Pentecostal churches that had not seen a revival since the 1950's when two missionaries came from the United States.

If ever I needed to know that the power of the Holy Spirit was with me, it was on this trip. How do you bring a fresh move of the Holy Spirit to a people who have stayed faithful in building on a tradition established fifty years ago?

We had no idea what we were getting ourselves into for this trip. We were two Americans who knew nothing of their traditions or their approach to ministry. We were sent there to do a work and so we carried on as if we were in any other city.

The first night of meetings was met with great apprehension as everyone looked at us with questionable "holiness." We found out very soon that in their church culture women did not wear makeup, jewelry or—God forbid—pants.

Cherrie's history includes winning several beauty pageants, including runner up in the Mrs. America Pageant, as well as being a model and spokesperson for several Fortune 500 companies. She is also a certified Executive and Live Coach. Though she does not dress to the extreme or overemphasize makeup at all, her very appearance brought a strange silence in the church.

What the people of Imperatriz soon found out was that she would be used of God to melt the heart of the church and usher in a new chapter in the life of the churches and the denomination.

And then there was me, a bearded preacher, a no-suit-or tie guy who loves to wear Tommy Bahama shirts and grow his hair a little long. We were to find out later that in another group of Assembly of God churches in Brazil, it was a written doctrine in their churches that men could not have beards and must wear ties when entering the house of God. It would be an understatement to say we had missed protocol. If I ever needed the impartation that had occurred in my life to be activated, it was now!

That night I preached a message about the need for the power of God to come and release revival. Afterwards I called for anyone that needed healing to come forward. As people began to make their way forward for prayer, a young mother came straight toward me with her daughter in tow. I soon found out her daughter was born deaf. As I prayed for her, the little girls eyes began to gaze around the room with a wide-eyed look. Her mother signed to her and asked her if she could hear. She signed back, "Yes!" Her mother began to cry and we were in awe. I asked if she would go to the platform and give testimony to what Jesus had just done for her and her daughter. As the mother began to speak, the reserved tradition within the church began to give way to a new sense of awe as Heaven was released among us.

It was a setup! God knew how to get the wonderful people of that church to look beyond their tradition and begin to open their hearts to receive all that He had for them. It was amazing!

During the month that followed, there was an impartation and activation of healing with the pastors and churches that went beyond all our expectations. Toward the end of our stay, one of the leaders, with tears streaming down his face, told me that he finally realized it was all about the Holy Spirit and not about the way someone dressed or looked. Not once did we talk about their tradition, we simply loved them and displayed the presence of God.

As we waited at the airport for our departing flight, the president of the denomination and his wife approached my wife with tears in their eyes and said, "We were an army but we forgot one thing: we didn't demonstrate our love to the people. You came and cried with us, prayed for us and hugged us and even kissed the feet of many of our people. We will never be the same. Your love for us has changed our city."[26]

Cherrie carries a true and passionate love for the people of Imperatriz and the Indian Tribe. She would wake up in the night and stand at our hotel room window, which overlooked the city, praying and interceding for the people. She would hug and embrace them. The kiss on the cheeks and on the feet of the people

---

[26] Romans 2:4 (author's paraphrase): "It is the kindness of God that leads to repentance (change)."

dismantled the wall of tradition. When the power of God swept through the churches, they had been prepared by a love that melted their hearts and created a hunger for more of God.

While in Imperatriz we met a family of missionaries from America who had been ministering to a Brazilian Indian tribe for over 30 years. David and Diane Bailey, along with their family, had remained faithful to the call of God but were at a place where they were ready to call it quits. We met them through their son David Jr., who owned an English School in Imperatriz. David had been asked to translate for us during the meetings. The Bailey's were a part of a very conservative organization that did not allow them to discuss the things of the Holy Spirit with the tribe. After years of service, the fruit that was produced amounted to around six villagers coming to Christ and meeting for Bible study.

One of the topics I was teaching on was the operation of Words of Knowledge as described in 1 Corinthians 12:8: "For to one is given the word of wisdom through the Spirit, and to another the word of knowledge according to the same Spirit."

My translator, David Jr., decided that he wanted this gift to operate in his life. So one day at the school, he asked God for a word of knowledge. To his amazement, he received an accurate word for someone in his class. David Jr. was so excited; he couldn't wait to share the testimony that the work of the Holy Spirit was real! After hearing and experiencing the move of the Holy Spirit in his life, he called his parents and asked them to come to the city and attend the meetings.

David Sr. and his wife Diane came at their son's suggestion. What they began to see and hear brought them to a place of searching the Scriptures to see if what they were experiencing was true. They said they couldn't find anything that would lead them to believe the message and the signs weren't from God. Diana was so hungry that she would come to our hotel and sit with Cherrie saying, "Please talk. Teach me. Teach me anything you want."

David Sr. told me later that in 1994 he had had an encounter with God but that he had "put it on the shelf." Now, after being around the fresh move of the Holy Spirit, he would never allow it to stop in his life again. This family received such an impartation of fire and joy that they soon resigned from the conservative missionary organization. Not knowing what would happen next, they stepped out in faith and like a page in a book turning, their life in the village took a radical shift.

We returned to Imperatriz two years later and found that the converts in the village had increased from six to 250 and were still growing! The power of God was falling in the meetings and people were being healed. They had experienced a revival of repentance—they were asking their peers for forgiveness, something that is unheard of in their culture! This repentance transformed the tribe and many were healed. The Indian tribe, on their own initiative, pooled their money to rent transportation to

travel to other villages to share the message of Jesus and pray for those who were sick.
During one night meeting in the village, a group of Indians chose to stay away and worship their "traditional" animal gods. As they looked down on the place where the other villagers were worshiping God they saw a bright light like a ball of fire. They ran down to see what was going on because they thought the group was setting off fireworks. When they got there, they saw people worshiping Jesus and laying on the ground. They realized that the ball of light was not fireworks but something they had never seen before. It frightened them so much they all ran back to their huts without finishing their own pagan rituals!

The stories of what God is doing in this area of Brazil will fill a book entirely on their own. When revival comes it overtakes anyone who is hungry and thirsty for more of God. The cry for more is always answered.

In Imperatriz we also ministered at a church called New Alliance Church. The pastor had recently been filled with the Holy Spirit and had to leave the denomination because the ministry of the Holy Spirit was not accepted. When he left, there were four hundred people who went with him. I ministered to this new group of hungry believers and the Holy Spirit showed up for them in such power that they where asking if this is what the Toronto Blessing looked like. It was an amazing night for all of us. This had never happened to them and it did look like the Toronto Blessing in many ways.

Two years after the first initial ministry trip to Imperatriz, we returned to find that New Alliance Church had grown to over 1,500 people, the youth group exploded from thirty students to three hundred, and they needed to find a new place to meet because they couldn't contain everyone who wanted to come!

The New Alliance church and the Indian village have now joined together for training, support, and advancement of revival in their region.

The denominational churches had grown from 108 to 124, and were embracing into the churches people from the region. They had grown from thirty thousand to about fifty thousand. Many of the leaders began to do and teach what we had shown them. One excited leader told me that he just returned from a crusade he had conducted and he taught the same message I had taught. He said, "It works! Many people were healed and I received many Words of Knowledge."

During the first trip Cherrie prayed for a lady who had a tumor in her breast. As she was praying, the tumor disappeared. This lady was so transformed that she began to hold healing crusades herself. During her meetings, she told us that God told her to pray specifically for sugar diabetes. He told her that as she prayed to turn the wrist of the person over. She was to watch as the veins in the arm would rise and fall back to normal. This would be a sign that the sugar diabetes was healed. On our return trip she told us that over six hundred people had received the "sign" and were healed!

Does the impartation of fire and power make a difference in our life? The answer is a strong "Yes!" These testimonies are a direct result of the activation of the Holy Spirit's power through the ministry of impartation and a willingness to release it to others.[27]

Again, I want to encourage you to go for more. There is an endless supply of undiscovered places and experiences with God. His desire to reveal more of His amazing love is never ending. And He wants you to experience His kingdom in your life right now.

"Heavenly Father, I pray right now for a fresh baptism of Your love. Fill me now with love for Your people. Let me see those around me through Your eyes. Increase the foundation of Your love in my life and the display of Your power and wonders that I would know You like I've never known You before."

---

[27] Mark 16:20: "And they went out and preached everywhere, while the Lord worked with them, and confirmed the word by the signs that followed."

Chapter 5

Voyage To Vision

...your young men
will see visions.
— Acts 2:17 (NIV)

"The real voyage of discovery consists
of not in seeking new landscapes
but in having new eyes."
Marcel Proust

When I was twelve years old my favorite show to watch on television was Voyage to the Bottom of the Sea. It was a science fiction show about a crew on board a submarine that met with different challenges and dangers each week. It fell right in line with my adventurous nature as I too fought monsters, giant octopus, and other strange creatures. The only difference between the submarine crew and me was that they had a television set on which to pursue their noblest adventures and I had a farm.

One of the biggest obstacles I had to overcome in order to watch the show was that Voyage to the Bottom of the Sea was broadcast on Sunday nights. My family and I attended Sunday evening classes called "Training Union" at our local Baptist church. I will have to confess, there were several times that I felt "too sick" to go with the rest of my family. So mom and dad would let me stay home while they, along with my brother and sister, went ahead to the evening church service. But like a miraculous form of medicine, every time I heard the car drive away, I suddenly was able to jump up out of bed, with no symptom of a stomachache or headache whatsoever. It was as if some miracle had befallen me. I would tell myself, "Since I am feeling better now, I'm sure mom and dad will not mind me watching Voyage to the Bottom of the Sea." So I would compose myself and turn the TV to my favorite show and watch with one ear to the show and one ear to the driveway.

Needless to say, my sickness soon became suspect to my parents. They would often tell me to just come along with them because they somehow knew I would feel better once I got to church. And you know, they were right. It was during one of those evening classes that I received my first visitation of the Holy Spirit in the form of an open vision.

I was sitting in a greenish-blue room in the basement of the church. The room was filled with other kids my age and we were totally bored out of our gourd. I would just sit there and look around the room trying to endure the lecture from some older gentlemen (whom I am sure was very good at what he did but I just wasn't interested). As I was glancing around the room counting the minutes till class was over, the wall directly in front of me began to change. My eyes became fixed and suddenly the sounds in the room fell silent. Out of nowhere, like someone pressing through the wall from the other side, a cross appeared on the wall. I froze! I was in shock and could not move. I wanted desperately to jump up and yell, "Look at that!" but I couldn't move. I sat quietly while everything inside of me was in hyper drive: "Where did that come from? What does it mean?"[28]

As suddenly as the cross appeared, it disappeared. I was left feeling very puzzled, questioning what had just happened. My heart was beating a thousand times a minute. I was only twelve and I had just been confronted with my first taste of a different reality, another

---

[28] Acts 2:17: "In the last days, God says, I will pour out my Spirit on all people. … your young men will see visions…"

dimension. It was like something from the Twilight Zone. An unseen realm had literally invaded my world! My heart was awakened to the truth that there was more to what is around us than what we can see with our eyes or feel with our hands. I will have to admit, as good as Voyage To The Bottom of The Sea was, seeing that cross appear was the first experience that sent me on a quest for the reality of the supernatural for the rest of my life.

Early that same year, I was walking in my backyard with a deep hunger for the supernatural, for more of the reality of God. I knew there was more to life than what I had been experiencing. As I read the stories in the Bible of the Old Testament prophets, they became like super heroes to me. Out of my heart I prayed this deeply sincere prayer, "Lord, give me faith like the prophets." I have no idea where that desire came from or how it even got into my heart. I meant that prayer with every ounce of my being. God heard my prayer and began to cultivate that desire in me.

One of my favorite heroes of the Bible was Elisha. When I was younger, my heart would burn with hunger as I read his story in the Bible. When I would read about floating ax heads and calling down fire from Heaven, I would dream of being used by God in such astounding ways.

And what about Samuel? If God would speak to a young boy named Samuel, then why wouldn't He speak to me? Surely if the Lord would strengthen a young man named David to kill a giant, He would surely use me too.

These thoughts and aspirations were a normal part of my life. My home was a place where the Lord was discussed and talked about day after day. I was born into a family with spiritual destiny. My father, called to preach, would also fill our home with amazing songs of worship, as he and my mom would sing about the things of the Lord.

My Grandpa Alexander was a minister all of his life until he went home to be with the Lord at the age of one hundred. I remember hearing stories of him going to Arizona to minister to the Navajo Indians and conducting camp meetings where songs of worship were sung, the Word was preached, and people were brought to salvation. Even in his later years he would rise each morning and give the first portion of his day in study and worship to the Lord.

One morning during breakfast, when I was five or six, I remember Grandpa Alexander teaching me to sing the song, "Fishers of Men," in the Navajo language. Later on I learned that my grandpa was a friend of William Branham who also ministered to Native Americans in the West. They both ministered and lived in the same town and at times would be together in their quest for the Kingdom.

The call of God on my family, on my life, was something that God was beginning to reveal to me. In His timing, He began to draw me into more of a living reality and life- giving relationship with Him by revealing Himself to me through the simple yet profound open vision of a cross.

The God of the Bible stories that I would read had made Himself known to me. He was alive, very real, and wanted to be involved in my life.

"Lord, I pray that You would bring to my recall any events in my life where You were speaking to me and reaching to me. Help me to see the visions of destiny in my life and the resolve of knowing that You have always been with me and have my best interest at heart. Open my eyes to see."

Chapter 6

Dream Encounters

In a dream, in a vision of the night,
When sound sleep falls upon men,
While they slumber in their beds,
Then He opens the ears of men,
And seals their instruction...
— Job 33:15-16

"A dream which is not interpreted is
like a letter which is not read."
~The Talmud

My life on the farm was kind of laid back except when there were chores to do, and that was most of the time. I didn't mind the work. I knew it was part of what sustained my family. This was our home. The place my brother Roy and sister Lillian and myself grew up. The farm and my family were my places of solitude and escape.

We believed that serving God and building family were the most important things in life. We knew that in honoring family we were establishing a foundation that would lead us into a greater realm of serving God. So we always had aunts, uncles and relatives coming by for a visit, or stopping by so we could spend time together. We were not the perfect family by far, but we knew what it meant to stick together.

My Grandma Caylor (my father changed the spelling to Kaylor) was a contrary but unwavering soul who had weathered a tough life in the South. She lived with us in a home in a small town called Athens located in rural eastern Tennessee. She was a lively character and always seemed to be mad at someone or something. I honestly believe that it was the pain of losing her husband, Lossie Fout Caylor, at a young age that broke her heart and left her lonely and unable to deal with life. Life was hard. Raising five children on your own in those times was a miraculous feat in and of itself. Building a hard shell around her heart was apparently the only way she knew how to protect herself and survive.

I remember one day when I was a young boy, being chased around the backyard by her with a switch in hand. If you are not from Tennessee or somewhere in the South, a "switch" is a flexible limb of a plant that when smacked across bare legs hurts like the dickens. It was used to give a spanking when a spanking was called for. Sometimes Grandma Caylor would get mad at me and then make me go and get my own switch from the garden!

Well, one day she was upset for some reason and she thought I had done something I did not do. So she told me to go and get a switch. On the way to and from the garden I was determined that there was no way I was going to be switched for something I did not do. If you looked just right you could find switches that were so thin that they would break in half after the first swat, especially if you were wearing long pants. On that particular day I happened to be wearing jeans so I wasn't too concerned about it. But this time, after mulling it over in my mind, it was the principle of the situation that was bugging me. I was being accused of something I did not do. So I decided I would stand up to her. And so I did.

Without even the least bit of forewarning, she began to turn redder than any fire truck I had ever seen. The scariest thing about it was that she suddenly stopped talking! I knew then I was in trouble. The very meaning of the word "switchin" was about to be redefined. In a flash, in the blink of an eye, the reason why my nickname became "fleet foot" was born. To my astonishment, and

I'm sure hers, I was suddenly transported from standing in front of her to a faint speck on her glasses followed by a trail of dust. I had escaped with my "principle" still intact.

One late evening when I was fourteen, I fell asleep for the night, just as I had done every night before. But this night was to change my understanding of hearing the voice of God. As I was sleeping I had a dream. In the dream I was lying on my bed and was awakened by loud crying coming from the kitchen. As I lay there, more sobs joined in and I became afraid. What has happened? What is going on? Suddenly, my bedroom door was opened and my father came and stood at the foot of my bed. He stared at me, but said nothing. And I watched as his expression turned to great sorrow. Then he just turned and walked away with tears running down his cheeks. Then I heard a voice that said, "Your grandmother has passed away."

I suddenly woke up and shot right up out of my bed. I sat there as quiet as I could, listening for someone crying or talking, but there was nothing but silence. I got out of bed and walked through the house but no one was awake and nothing was unusual. I thought to myself, "I have had a nightmare," so I went back into my room and lay back down and went to sleep. I woke up the next day, not saying anything to anyone about my dream. After breakfast I headed off to school. But I could not shake the impact of the dream off. It was as real as the day.

Two weeks later, after going to bed and dozing off to sleep for the night I was at once awakened by the sound of crying and sorrow. From that point on, the dream that

I had two weeks earlier began to replay, but this time it was real. From the sounds of crying in the house to my dad walking into my room to him leaving my room, it all played over like a bad dream. But this time, waking up would not stop the nightmare, because my dream was becoming a reality.

The shock of losing my grandma began to give way to the unexplained question of how I knew this was going to happen. Down to the last detail, I had foreseen an event that had not yet happened! I again found myself in a place of bewilderment. It did not take long for me to understand that it was the Lord who had spoken to me through a dream, but I was confused about why He would speak to me in such a way. After all, I was told at church that God only speaks through the Bible today.

The Bible is filled with stories of people having dreams, but I just read over them like they where some kind of fantasy that had no place in the world today. However, this encounter with God through a dream began a new chapter in my life as I started to understand that the dream world is a valid avenue in which God speaks to us today.

For example, I had known that God had a unique destiny for my life but it was a dream that confirmed it. When I was twenty-one years old, I was awakened from a dream with a message that would unfold to me a specific path and direction for my life.

In the dream I was sitting on a wooden bench in the back of a very large cathedral-type church, like those found in Europe. As I was sitting there I could overhear people talking about the sons of God. Suddenly a hand with a finger pointing directly to my face appeared. Then I heard, *"It is in Zechariah 3:7."* It startled me so much that I instantly woke up and turned on the light in my bedroom. I walked over and picked up my Bible to try and find the book of Zechariah. I knew it was in the Old Testament but I had never read it and knew nothing about it. When I found it I immediately turned to chapter 3 and verse 7.

The first few words made me step back and catch my breath as my eyes filled with tears. *"Thus says the LORD of hosts."* The God of creation was speaking face to face, as it were, with me. A twenty-one year old guy who had no clue to the direction for his life. God was talking to me. He was very much alive and real! As I continued to read it said,

> *"If you will walk in My ways and if you will perform My service, then you will also govern My house and also have charge of My courts, and I will grant you free access among these who are standing here." Zach:3;7*

This was the beginning point in my life where the voice of God through dreams became a valuable and important part of my spiritual understanding. Dreams became a very distinct way in which God would speak to me. It became such a part of my life that is a joy to help unlock this channel of communication for others. I enjoy greatly teaching our seminars on how God uses dreams to speak to us. I have written a dream curriculum that we use in our ministry school entitled Dreams: Unveiling The Voice of God.

Recently a minister that I knew fell into sin. I asked the Lord if I should contact him as it had been years since we had talked. That night I had a dream in which five numbers appeared on the side of a mailbox. When I woke up I knew the numbers where a zip code. I immediately went to my computer and put the five numbers into Google search. A link for a region of the country came up. When I clicked on the link a map appeared. In the center of the map a road with the same name as my friend appeared. God had answered me.

I would encourage you to ask God to speak to you through your dreams. They are a foundational way He communicates with us. Dreams were the central form of direction during one of the most important events in history: the birth of Jesus.[29]

I have found there are a few things that can be done to help you remember and interpret the dreams you know are from the Lord.

First, keep a journal by your bed. It could be in the form of a pad and pencil or a digital or tape recorder. As soon as you wake up record the dreams of the night. Write them in as much detail as you can for each item in the dream because those details might play a part in the message of the dream.

---

[29] Matthew 1:20; 2:12-13, 19, 22

Second, ask the Holy Spirit for the meaning. It is important to know that most dreams are symbolic in nature. The symbols or items in the dream represent something that is pulled from the life of the dreamer.

Third, close your eyes and meditate on the dream, remembering as much detail as you can. What do the symbols represent to you? For example, if you dream of being in your home, you may be receiving direction concerning your inner life, your internal person. Or you may have dreamed of driving your car. This could represent the direction your life has taken or is going to take. If you are in the passenger seat, the dream may be telling you that you are not in control of your life or where it is going.

These are just a few ideas that may help you in getting started in recording your dream life. Remember that God always desires to speak with us. Learning how to hear through various avenues enables us to be in a position to always be listening.

"Father, I ask that Your voice would be made known to me and the dreams and visions of the night be made clear. I am asking that Your Spirit of wisdom and revelation would increase so that I may know Your voice in the dreams which are divinely inspired. Thank You for giving understanding to the interpretation and symbols and events in my dreams as Your love continues to guide me. I just want to say I love You too."

Chapter 7

I'm Floating!

...whether in the body I do not know,
or out of the body I do not know, God knows
—such a man was caught up...
— 2 Corinthians 12:2

"We are not human beings having a spiritual experience.
We are spiritual beings having a human experience."
Pierre Teilhard de Chardin

I had just graduated from high school and was looking forward to going to college. It was the 70's during the summer months between high school and college, I spent a lot of time practicing with my band and hanging out with my friends. Some friends and I had put together a Christian rock band and we were very excited to see where God would take us. It was a slightly different time then—many churches in the Southern United States just couldn't get past the idea of having drums in church, much less guys with long hair. We had our share of name calling and shut doors, but God was faithful and launched us out on a wonderful adventure, traveling through the United States, bringing evangelism through preaching the gospel and playing culture current music.

During the summer of that year I was at a friend's home in the afternoon and we were sitting around trying to decide on something to do. It was hot, we were bored, so what else would one do except pray? Yeah right! My friend had suggested that we pray. To be honest, praying was the last thing on my mind. In fact, I tried to suggest something else for us to do but with nothing else sounding good, we decided to go ahead and pray. He said, "I will pray first and then you can pray." It was just the two of us in the living room, so I agreed. While he was praying, I bowed my head and began to think, "Great, I don't feel like praying, much less know what to pray. I can't even think of anything to pray about." Needless to say, I wasn't burning with excitement.

When he was done, it was my turn. What happened next is hard to even put into words. With no real intention of praying or expecting anything to happen, I took a deep breath and began to open my mouth and pray. Suddenly I found myself being lifted straight up and out of my chair. Apparently the ceiling of the house presented no obstacle to this flight I had just embarked on. I kept looking, and when I gazed down I could see my friend in his house sitting in his chair with his eyes closed still praying. As I lifted my eyes to look around I found myself engulfed with a transparent whiteness. It was like being in a cloud. I was so startled by the fact I was floating that I became afraid and I suddenly found myself sitting back in the chair in the house again.

"What had just happened?" I said to myself. I had never experienced anything like that. As I sat there quietly, I began to realize I had just had some type of spiritual encounter. Was it the Holy Spirit? Was it an angel? I was not sure. But one thing I was sure about—it was good. I felt refreshed. I was spiritually energized. Although I couldn't find the words to explain what had just happened, I knew that a divine download from Heaven had taken place within me. Maybe it was the "calling" I had heard about so much in our church. I knew my father was "called" into the ministry and also my grandfather. Was I now next in line for "the call"?

As I played this experience over and over in my mind, I remembered something I had asked the Lord several months earlier. Our band was practicing in the basement of a local church. As I was leaving, I walked outside and with a hungry heart asked God, "Is this all there is to church?" I was so tired of lifeless routine. I read the stories of the disciple's great exploits and it made me burn inside. I wanted to experience and live what they had lived. I was desperate, but nothing in my church even hinted at this type of life.

Once again, I believe my simple prayer caught the ear of God. He opened my eyes, even if for a moment, to allow me to know that there was a greater reality than what I was experiencing. A taste of His presence made me even more determined to receive all that He had to give. It felt like a flame had been lit on the inside of me and this taste of the heavenly experiences caused my hunger to increase.

In thinking about this experience, I can't help but wonder if this is what Paul talked about in 2 Corinthians 12:2*: "I know a man in Christ who fourteen years ago was caught up to the third heaven. Whether it was in the body or out of the body I do not know—God knows…"*

In this verse Paul makes reference to being "caught up." I do not believe I was taken to the third Heaven but there was a definite "catching up."

Another story that comes to mind is the story of Philip:

> *As they traveled along the road, they came to some water and the eunuch said, "Look, here is water. Why shouldn't I be baptized?" And he gave orders to stop the chariot. Then both Philip and the eunuch went down into the water and Philip baptized him. When they came up out of the water, the Spirit of the Lord suddenly took Philip away, and the eunuch did not see him again, but went on his way rejoicing. Philip, however, appeared at Azotus and traveled about, preaching the gospel in all the towns until he reached Caesarea* (Acts 8:36-40, NIV).

There was obviously a transition of dimensional time and space. Philip was transported out of his tangible position with the eunuch through some type of spiritual portal and he landed in Azotus.

Jesus was "taken up" as He ascended into Heaven after His resurrection:

> *After he said this, he was taken up before their very eyes, and a cloud hid him from their sight. They were looking intently up into the sky as he was going, when suddenly two men dressed in white stood beside them. "Men of Galilee," they said, "why do you stand here looking into the sky? This same Jesus, who has been taken from you into heaven, will come back in the same way you*

> *have seen him go into heaven"* (Acts 1:9-11, NIV).

We understand that the realms of earth—time and space—are all subject to the laws of the higher realm of God's kingdom. The unfolding discoveries in Quantum Physics seem to have taken a giant step forward in actually seeing the inner workings of the spiritual world. How this type of dual dimensional life works is not something I need to understand before I believe that it operates. All I know is that it happens and it is real. If one day you find yourself being "beamed up" into a place that is not where you are physically standing, know that it is not an uncommon occurrence in the supernatural realm of the Kingdom of God.

"Father, I want more of You. More of Your Kingdom—more of Your unexplainable surprises. I am ready for an encounter that will awaken in me new depths of desire and passion. I want to walk with You like Enoch walked with You. Change the way I understand and know things. Let it come Lord. Let it come to me."

Chapter 8

Stop! I Can't Take Anymore!

Then those who sing as well as
those who play the flutes shall say,
"All my springs of joy are in you."
— Psalm 87:7

"If there is no laughter, Jesus has gone somewhere else. If there is no joy and freedom, it is not a church: it is simply a crowd of melancholy people basking in a religious neurosis. If there is no celebration, there is no real worship." - Steve Brown

I grew up in a home filled with music. My dad was a musician. Many times my dad, mom, and my relatives would get together to sing and play for hours. My grandfather was known as the "Singing Evangelist." I even have a picture of my great-grandfather playing his fiddle.

Music has been a part of my family legacy as far back as the Revolutionary War. My great (x6)-grandfather was a soldier in George Washington's brigade. Not only was he a rifleman, but he was also the fifer for the brigade. If you've ever seen the picture of the drummer, the flag carrier, and the fife player marching together, then you've seen a representation of my relative.

I remember seeing my dad come to life every time he picked up his guitar and began to play. Though he was a guitarist for Roy Acuff, the father of the Grand Ole Opry, he decided not to go down that path. My dad became content with recording a few albums, writing songs, playing at home or church, and spending time raising a family.

This same passion for music was passed on to me, an inheritance for which I am very grateful. I began playing the guitar when I was twelve years old. A few years later I joined my first rock band. I loved playing the songs of the day, but the Holy Spirit compelled me to commit my talent to serving Jesus.

In answer to that compulsion, two of my friends and I began what was one of the first contemporary Christian bands in the Southeastern United States. At that time the thought of playing contemporary music in a church was unheard of. It was hard to walk into a church with a beard and long hair, much less a full set-up that included amps, speakers, and (God forbid) drums.

While I was a part of this band I had an encounter that is as real to me now as it was years ago when I first experienced it. It was during a tour in the New Jersey and New York area. We had been asked to come and minister at a Baptist Youth Convention and share what the Lord had been doing in our lives as well as in our music. The meetings were located on a college campus and so we stayed in the dormitory.

The band, which at this time had five members, sat in a circle on the floor of the dorm room and enjoyed spending time in prayer and worship. And as we began, I started to sense something come over me that was as real as the rain outside. I suddenly felt a wonderful flow of power bubble up from deep inside of me. As it poured over my lips, the force became uncontrollable, unrestrained laughter.[30] At that moment I was thinking,

---

30 Psalm 126:2: "Our mouths were filled with laughter, our tongues
with songs of joy." See also Psalm 47:1; 68:3; 126:3.
Isaiah 12:3: "With joy, you will draw waters from the well of salvation."
Romans 14:17: "The kingdom of God is…joy in the Holy Spirit."

"This is the most awesome feeling I think I have ever had!" I was filled with joy and indescribable peace. Oswald Chambers recorded in his diary on April 19, 1907:

> *Last night we had a blessed time. I was called down by the teachers to pray and anoint a lady who wanted healing, and as we were doing it God came so near that upon my word we were laughing as well as praying! How utterly stilted we are in our approach to God. Oh that we lived more up to the light of all our glorious privileges.*[31]

A.W. Tozer also writes about unrestrained laughter, stating:

> *I once saw a man kneel at an altar, taking Communion. Suddenly he broke into holy laughter. This man laughed until he wrapped his arms around himself as if he was afraid he would bust just out of sheer delight in the presence of Almighty God.*[32]

As this encounter continued, I began to beat the floor with my hands and roll around in laughter. The experience was so intense that I finally cried out, "Stop!

Lord, I don't know if I can take anymore!" As I said that, the experience started to lift off of me. I was able to sit up, catch my breath, and shake my head in wonder.

---

[31] Oswald Chambers: His Life and Work

[32] A. W. Tozer, Worship: The Missing Jewel

Then suddenly, it began all over again! This went on for quite a while and was beyond anything I could have ever imagined. It was a new expression of the "hilarious" love of God being deposited in my life. I had been made to laugh hysterically by my loving Father who was playing with his son. I truly felt embraced.

The next morning we received a loud knock on our door. The Director of the youth meetings said he wanted to talk with us. He began by asking about all of the noise coming from our room the previous night. He told us the kids in the other dorm rooms came out and stood in the hall by our door to listen to whatever was happening. We just stood there and said we were praying together and worshipping the Lord. That was when he looked me square in the eyes and said, "I know exactly what happened in here and you'd better not tell anyone about it." "But what about explaining it to all of the kids?" I asked. "No. I will take care of it," he said. So we said, "Okay."

To be honest, everything inside of me wanted to gather everyone into a room and tell them what an awesome experience I just had. If kids wanted to get high on drugs, I was confident that once they tasted the presence of the Holy Spirit, they would never go back to their old lifestyle. I was so excited, and every rebellious ounce of me was drooling to go behind his back to share my experience with the kids. But I knew better. My parents raised me to be honorable and respectful, so I waited until a more opportune moment revealed itself.

Well, come to find out, the Youth Director had been part of a Pentecostal church. The church he was with now did not believe in the moves of the Holy Spirit. In fact, this church taught that things of this nature came from the devil. He simply did not want to run the risk of losing his job.

So what did I do with this new experience? It was amazing! The following account by Charles Finney brings a sense of confirmation and excitement concerning my particular encounter with God.

> *The Holy Ghost descended on me in a manner that seemed to go through me, body and soul. I could feel the impression, like a wave of electricity, going through and through me. Indeed it seemed to come in waves and waves of liquid love, for I could not express it in any other way. It seemed like the very breath of God. I can recollect distinctly that it seemed to fan me, like immense wings. No words can express the wonderful love that was shed abroad in my heart. I wept aloud with joy and love; and I do not know but I should say, I literally bellowed out the unutterable gushing of my heart. The waves came over me, and over me, one after the other, until I recollect I cried out, "I shall die if these waves continue to pass over me." I said, "Lord, I*

cannot bear any more;" yet I had no fear of death.[33]

If life at times seems to overwhelm you, sometimes it is good just to throw your head back and laugh. Laugh until you sense a breakthrough. Laugh until you can't stand up. Though it may not be considered "Spirit-birthed," it will help shake off the feelings of discouragement or depression that may come your way. And who's to say it is not Spirit-inspired? If you ever find yourself in a situation where you feel something beginning to bubble up inside of you, let it out! Don't hold back. It will refresh you in ways nothing else can.

Here is God's prescription: Proverbs 17:22 (KJV):

"A merry heart doeth good like a medicine…"

"Once again Lord, I am asking for a refreshing in my life. A lifestyle of laughter and joy to fill me as I walk with You during our journey. Lord, let Your joy be made full and overflowing. May my soul prosper with outrageous joy as You capture my heart again. Come Holy Spirit. Come upon me now."

[33] Autobiography of Charles Finney

Chapter 9

Changed Forever

Receive the Holy Spirit.
John 20:22

"Come Holy Spirit. Let the power come!"
John Wimber

Shortly after my experience in the dorm room I met a very prominent businessman and minister named Norvel Hayes. Norvel ministered all over the world and he asked if our Christian band would come and minister at a coffeehouse he owned. Over the summer we ministered many times at his coffeehouse in Cleveland, Tennessee. It was a place where people came to give and receive prayer.

One day Norvel asked if we would come with him and lead worship for the youth at the Regional Full Gospel Business Men's Convention in Nashville. I had never heard of the organization before, but we were excited for a place to minister. On the first day of the conference there were the typical announcements before beginning worship. At that time my worship expression was in need of a higher level of experience.

As the songs began, my heart started to connect with the sound of the music. It was something I had never felt before. There was a deep pulling in my spirit to let go and sing with all my might. The songs seemed to flow from one to the next without any pause or fanfare in between. We did not have a set song list to follow nor a clock to be concerned about. It was a new way of worship that grabbed me and wouldn't let me go. And I didn't want it too. My eyes were closed and my heart was soaring. As the song ended I heard something coming from the back of the auditorium. I stood there, my mind racing with the possibility that what I was hearing was a song of the angels. It was the most beautiful sound I had ever heard. It kept getting louder and louder and it was moving in my direction. What was this? I was almost afraid to open my eyes for fear of what I might see. Angels? This had to be an angelic visitation.

As the song swept over the entire audience, I decided I would open my eyes and take a look at the source of the song. When I looked around I saw hundreds and hundreds of people singing the song that I was listening to but with no directions or particular lyrics. "What is going on?" I thought. "How can everyone be singing with such lyrical unity?" The melodic tones were layered together like a piece of orchestral music.[34]

After the service I went to Norvel and asked him about the beautiful song. That was when I found out about something I was told was not supposed to happen in our day and time. He told me that everyone was "singing in the spirit." Or more plainly put, "singing in tongues." Without any hesitation I asked him how I could get "tongues"? I wanted to be able to worship as those who were around me were worshipping. Norvel laid his hands on me to pray for the gift of tongues—an act that started this wonderful journey of walking, praying, singing, and living in a new realm of God: the realm of the Baptism of the Holy Spirit.[35]

Soon after I began to receive more experiences with God, including new dimensions of understanding

---

[34] 1 Corinthians 14:15

[35] Act 11:16

regarding Scripture. It was like I was reading the Bible for the first time. Something was changing deep inside of me.

A few weeks later we were driving through St. Louis very late one night while on tour through the Midwest. I was lying on the floor of our touring vehicle and began to pray with the new language I had received. It was so amazing to speak in a language that was given to me and that I didn't have to study to learn. I had taken Latin, Spanish, and French in college and to this day I can't remember but a few words. So this was exciting! It was truly the supernatural in a daily expression of my life.

After praying for some time in the spirit, I began to feel a very heavy presence come over me. It was like something was lying on my chest. As the weight increased, so did the intensity of my prayer. I began to pray with a deep groaning I had never experienced before. The prayer seemed to grip my mouth and throat, and I knew what I was feeling was the very presence of God. With each word I tried to speak, I felt I was speaking in slow motion. It was terrifying and wonderful at the same time.

Without any doubt in my mind I knew that if I were to open my eyes, I would be before the throne of God itself. I knew that I was not alone in this experience. There were other beings in this place which I later came to realize were angels. The thought of angels was enough to jolt me back into reality. I felt myself return back inside the vehicle.

I was now aware of my surroundings once again. However, a deep yearning in my heart to understand what had just happened to me, and an overwhelming desire in me to experience more of this still remained. What was this new dimension that I felt I had entered?

The feeling of the "heaviness" was fantastic and perplexing. It was a sensation I will never forget.

The Hebrew word for glory, "kabod," means weight or heaviness. There is a tangible substance to the glory of God. It is His presence. Paul speaks of this in 2 Corinthians 4:17 when he refers to the exceeding and eternal weight of Glory.

Have you ever wondered why, in Acts 5:15, people would line up in the street so that Peter's shadow would pass over them? When Peter's shadow passed over the infirmed, it wasn't his shadow that contained power. It was the substance (or weight) of the presence of God Peter carried with him that touched and healed the people.

What about this verse? Acts 19:12[36] says that even handkerchiefs or aprons were carried from Paul's body to the sick, and the diseases left them and the evil spirits went out.

In 2 Chronicles 5:14[37] the priests were not able to stand and minister to the Lord because of the cloud of

---

[36] "So that even handkerchiefs and aprons that had touched him were taken to the sick, and their illnesses were cured and the evil spirits left them."

[37] "So that the priests could not continue ministering because of the cloud; for the glory of the LORD filled the house of God."

glory that filled the room. The word "cloud" in Hebrew means "something with mass." In other words, it is the substance of the presence or glory of God.

As I thought about this new experience, I knew that much of what I had learned in church about the activity of God in the Earth was simply not true. I have since learned that one tangible experience from God can remove years of bad theology. The Kingdom is more easily "caught" than "taught." Instead of trying to academically tell someone about the Holy Spirit, it is much easier to simply experience Him.

This baptism of the Holy Spirit did not begin a new chapter in my life—it began a new book! It was like a new path of communication had opened up between God and myself. When I would read the Word, truths began to jump off the page as if they had been buried in a forgotten archeological dig. My passion for spending time in prayer went off the charts. This new prayer language I had received made my former prayer time seem like kindergarten. I began to understand Paul when he said to pray without stopping. It was a joy to pray! Never had I had something change my life so dramatically.

As I looked into this new experience, I found out the book called "The Acts of The Apostles"[38] is the record of the works of the apostles after they had received the infilling of the Holy Spirit. This was the same Holy Spirit that now filled me. In a way, the book could have been

---

[38] The book is called "Acts" for short.

named "The Acts of the Holy Spirit" with the final chapter still waiting to be written.

If you have never received the Baptism of the Holy Spirit then you are in the right place at the right time for a life changing experience. Yes, it is true that you receive the Holy Spirit upon salvation,[39] but there is another experience with the Holy Spirit that activates power in and through your life.[40] The gift of tongues is a door to a life that is filled with supernatural expression.

Ask for the Holy Spirit to come and fill you anew. We need only ask for more. He will hear and answer. Be filled with the Holy Spirit! Be refreshed and empowered! Allow the language of the Spirit to flow over your lips and the power of His presence to bubble up inside of you. Ask Him to release a new dimension of His "living water" into your Life.[41] Through the pages of this book, we lay hands on you to receive a fresh baptism of the Holy Spirit!

Jesus said:

> *"Which of you fathers, if your son asks for a fish, will give him a snake instead? Or if he asks for an egg, will give him a scorpion? If you then, though you are evil, know how to give good gifts to your children, how much more will your Father in heaven give the Holy Spirit to those who ask him" !* (Luke 11:11-13).

[39] Ephesians 1:13

[40] Acts 1:8; 2:4; 19:2

[41] John 7:37

"Holy Spirit, I am asking that Your gifts ignite in me. That the heavenly languages begin to flow fresh in me. That You baptize me and fill me to overflowing. Let Your power flow into me and Your breathe fill my spirit, my soul, and my body. I take You at Your word, that when I ask for more, You will give it. Thank You! Pressed down, shaken together and running over, I receive a fresh impartation of Your Spirit!"

Chapter 10

Pray Him Out Of Town!

That set everyone in the meeting place seething with anger... but he gave them the slip and was on his way.

— Luke 4:28-20 (The Message)

After ministering around the United States, the band returned home for a short time. Coming home brought a new passion for the things of the Holy Spirit and the supernatural realm of God. I had developed such a hunger and love for the truths of how the Holy Spirit works in our lives, that it was all I could do to contain myself. However, my new passion brought with it an unexpected reaction in town.

My heart was toward the youth in our area and I decided I would go to the local high school and ask if I could have a time of Bible study for the students after school. To my delight I was given permission and was allowed to use the Art Department room before school for the meetings. I had been a student at the school before and was greatly involved with the Art Department during my high school years. My relationship with my art teacher was positive considering she felt I was one of her better students. Plus she was a Christian and attended one of the local Baptist churches. She was excited to see the students in the school receiving the gospel.

At our first meeting we had about ten students who showed up. It was exciting. I spoke about the Holy Spirit and the things I was experiencing. Before long, the group grew to about fifty students. It was awesome! I was so excited to see the hunger in everyone. And it wasn't just the "Jesus Freaks" who showed up. People who before had shown no interest in the things of God were now standing in the same room with those who grew up in church—the long hairs and the short hairs, the ties and the t-shirts, all together in this one room for one cause. It was as if a light had been turned on and everyone was being drawn towards it. No one could believe that serving Jesus could be fun or that you didn't have to look like the evangelists on television. God loved you and would use you just as you are.

One morning after our meeting, the art teacher said she needed to speak with me. She informed me the meetings would have to stop. No real explanation for why was given except that it would be best to not use her room anymore. So I decided that moving the meetings into some of the student's homes would be the best alternative.

With such short notice we were left without a place to meet. I decided to call the assistant pastor at the First Baptist church where I had attended when I was home to ask him if I could use the fellowship hall. The church building itself was a beautiful stone structure with towering white columns lining the entrance into the foyer. This was one of the prettiest places in town, so to use this facility would be awesome.

I explained to the assistant pastor that I was doing a series of Bible studies for the students and this week we were without a place to meet. "Well of course," he said. "Anything to help with the youth." I was really glad that he did not ask me what the topics were for our Bible study. Knowing the Baptist persuasion concerning the things of the Holy Spirit, he might have changed his mind.

The night for the Bible study came and we were all thrilled. The fellowship hall at the church was filling up quickly. However, I noticed that the assistant pastor was standing around in the back of the room checking everything out. It was time to start the meeting and since he was still in the room I began by speaking about the love of God. After a few moments he left—that was my cue. I moved from speaking about the love of God to the power of God through the Holy Spirit.

The youth in the room where so hungry for this "new" teaching that they were on the edge of their seats. Of course many of you understand that there is no "new thing" in God. Jesus was and will always be the "new thing." The Father was revealed through the Son. John states that so much was revealed about Jesus, the libraries of the world could not contain all that He did.[42] Everything Jesus said and did pointed towards the Father. Understanding this truth will help us stay grounded when we hear that God is doing a "new thing."

The "new" teaching I was giving the students was about the gifts of the Holy Spirit. This night the topic was to be on speaking in tongues and casting out demons. After spending time teaching, I gave them a testimony of a person with a demon being set free. This testimony came from a ministry trip I had taken with Norvel Hayes. We were in South Bend, Indiana, at Lester Sumrall's church where Norvel was about to give a message.

---

[42] John 21:25

For those of you who aren't familiar with Lester Sumrall, he was an amazing pastor and evangelist. At the age of seventeen he was suffering from tuberculosis and close to death. He then received a vision. Suspended in midair to the right of his bed was a casket. On the left side of the bed was a large open Bible. Then he heard these words: "Lester Sumrall, which of these will you choose tonight?" At that moment he committed his life to the preaching of the Gospel. When he awoke the next morning, he was totally and completely healed. His goal was to win one million souls for the Kingdom of God. He ministered in more than 110 countries and became the father of modern Christian television.

It was truly an honor to be in Lester's church. Norvel and Lester had shared the pulpit many times, but this was my first time to be with both of them.

As Norvel began to preach in Lester's church, everyone in the room became silent, listening with heightened expectation. As I was sitting and listening, I suddenly saw a women jump up out of her chair. She stood there for a minute and then began to scream at Norvel! She then made her way out of her seat into the aisle and headed straight to the front of the room. Norvel swung around and pointed his finger and locked eyes with her. The next thing he said was, "Stop, in the name of Jesus!" He then spoke to something or someone and told it to leave the woman and be gone. By this time I was in a frenzy wondering what was going on here. This had never happened in the church I grew up in!

The next thing I saw was the woman fall to the ground like someone had smacked her with a two-by-four. I thought to myself, "What in the world was going on here?" Then it hit me. The women had a demon! Not only that but Norvel cast it out of her and it was now loose somewhere in the room! I began to panic thinking it would come over and try to get in me! Then, with a soft, almost smiling voice, I heard the Holy Spirit say, "It's okay. It's gone and you have nothing to worry about." Whew! I had just seen my first bona-fide deliverance.

As I finished recounting this testimony, I could tell everyone was on the edge of their seat. This type of conflict and power was never mentioned in any of the Sunday school lessons or sermons these young people had heard. With excitement and momentum building in the room, I then lead them into being filled with the power of the Holy Spirit—the only power that could render useless the works of the enemy. As I lead them in prayer the students began to pray in the Holy Spirit. The room was charged with electricity. It's one thing to teach about the power of the Holy Spirit, but it is another thing to see His power in action and to experience it.

By now it was getting late and the parents were coming to pick up their kids. When the first parents entered the room to get their children, they got the strangest look on their faces. It wasn't the look I had hoped for. As the room cleared out I started to wonder if this night would make a difference in the young people as well as the church. As each one got into the car, they were inevitably asked the question, "What did you learn tonight at the Baptist youth Bible study?" It didn't take long before the parent's were in an uproar. After telling their parents they learned to speak in tongues and cast out demons the phone to the assistant pastor's office rang off the hook! After all, it was supposed to be a "Baptist" Bible study.

Needless to say we didn't meet at the church again and before long, it became difficult to find any home that would allow us to hold a Bible study. In fact, I was told that the parents were joining together and praying that I would leave town. Looking back, I am so glad God answered their prayers!

Once you taste the presence of the Lord in your life you will never be satisfied without it. One of the songs I have recently written, Your Presence, contains the following lyrics. It describes that continual hunger which has become an integral part of my life.

"Lord, you've brought me to

A place from which I will never return

For you have touched my heart

And now I hunger for more of you.

Deep within my soul

Now is a passion that always will burn

For you have filled me up

And yet I hunger for more of you.

Oh my God, you've ruined me

I will never be the same again,

The way I used to be

Oh my God you've ruined me

A hunger for Your presence now consumes me.

What can wash away the pain

The emptiness and the shame

Nothing oh nothing but Your presence

What will make me whole within

And fill my heart with joy again,

Nothing, oh nothing but Your presence."

Praying in the Holy Spirit or speaking in tongues should be a normal part of every Christian's life. For me, praying in the Holy Spirit became the doorway into a new realm of the supernatural things of God. Mysteries are revealed through praying in the Spirit. Faith is built[43] and destiny is set in motion by praying in the Holy Spirit.[44] If you've ever wondered if God hears your prayers, you can be sure this is the type of prayer that is always heard and always answered.

---

43 Jude 1:20

44 Romans 8:27; 1 John 5:14-15

Position yourself to receive. You have to build yourself up by praying in the Holy Spirit with the expectancy that what God has promised to do, He will do. To position yourself is to come to a place of internal surrender. It is a position of faith with expectation. Praying in the Holy Spirit helps us get to and stay in the place of internal grace so we can release the external witness of His power and love.

I encourage you to increase the time you spend praying in the Holy Spirit. If you have never experienced it, then simply ask Him for the gift of praying in the Holy Spirit. He will not take over your voice, nor will He overcome you, or come down and move your tongue for you. You must release your language through prayer or worship.

This will be new as with any language you may be speaking without understanding it at first. It may be like a child repeating a phrase the parent is saying to the child. The child is mimicking at first, but then begins to learn the language. Spiritual language is not any more complicated than natural language learning. The point of reference is the Lord fulfilling His Word in you and through you. As you begin to hear a change in your dialect, let it flow. Continue with it. Repeat it over and over if you wish. Or you can let it flow like a river with pause and inflection and perhaps accents until it becomes a part of you. The Scripture tells us the spirit is subject to the prophet.[45] The language of men and angels is subject to your voice in

[45] 1 Corinthians 14:32

order to bring it forth into this reality—Heaven coming to earth through you.

And don't be surprised if you suddenly have thoughts that this language is something you are making up—this is an old lie of the enemy. If you are giving an offering of praise or joyful noise to the Lord, and your affections and attentions are for an audience of one, just remember the sacrifice of praise always makes the enemy mad.

Speak out even more passionately and kick him a good one in the head. He is under your feet—and now even more so with the authority of the Holy Spirit in you. Remember, if you ask the Father for bread, He is not going to give you a stone. So as you've asked Him for this gift, He is faithful to give it to you.

Chapter 11

Divine Romance

He will send His angel before you,
and you will take a wife for my son...
— Genesis 24:7

"There are no coincidences in God."
– Bill Johnson

Does God have a plan for putting together partners for life? I believe He does. For instance, how could a boy from Eastern Tennessee meet and marry a beauty queen from Washington State? As we used to say "who'd a figured?"

For me, God's divine courtship started while touring the country doing evangelism through contemporary music. The band's brown overzealously converted UPS truck broke down in the little town called Goldendale, Washington. The location was beautiful. In the distance you could see snow capped mountains like Mount St. Helens and the picturesque Mount Hood.

It was winter and the amount of ice and snow on the roads and fields was beyond anything we had ever seen before. Considering that we were a group of guys from Tennessee, that isn't surprising. However, we suddenly found ourselves stranded in a strange town with no one to call for help.

Let me back track a bit. Being stranded was nothing new to us. This had happened one other time, but it was at the top of the Rocky Mountains in Colorado. We were lost on a back road with snow piled high on both sides when all of a sudden the van stopped dead in its tracks. We are musicians, not mechanics; but we thought we should at least take a look under the hood. We all stood and stared at the engine as if it was going to magically tell us what was wrong. The only thing we discovered was that it was close to zero degrees outside! The wind was blowing, making us look like red-cheeked chipmunks. Night was falling and all we knew to do was pray and huddle together, all five of us, under blankets in the back of the converted UPS truck.

After shivering through the night, morning came with a knock on the passenger's side of the van and a shout, "Anybody in there?" We scrambled from under the blankets to the door and to our relief it was a State Trooper. We told him what had happened and he proceeded to tell us that this is not a road he travels down often, but felt like he should drive down it this particular morning, especially since there was a murderer on the loose in the area! He called a tow truck for us and we soon found ourselves in a town that looked as if it had been frozen in time around the 1800's. It was amazing! It was a real cowboy town up in the mountains. While waiting for the garage to repair the van, we spent time in a restaurant straight out of one of those old Westerns, complete with swinging doors and a saloon. Before too long, the repair was complete and we found ourselves back on the road after a short stay in the 1800's.

On the surface, this event could be looked at as unusual, but a coincidental random occurrence. But what if it wasn't? What if there was a design to the overnight adventure that called into play an entire realm of unseen realities? Maybe this was the next step along the path of divine providence that was directing me.

As I began to think about this situation, I realized we were not alone that night on the cold mountain road. In fact, I believe there was an entire entourage of heavenly hosts laying claim to the protection of these five guys locked up shivering under blankets in the darkness of night. Psalm 91:9-12 says:

> *"For you have made the LORD, my refuge, even the Most High, your dwelling place. No evil will befall you, nor will any plague come near your tent. For He will give His angels charge concerning you, To guard you in all your ways. They will bear you up in their hands, that you do not strike your foot against a stone."*

How many coincidences of life are actually the unseen hand of God directing us step by step into the abounding plan He has for us?
The Bible says in Proverbs 3:5-6:

> *"Trust in the LORD with all your heart and do not lean on your own understanding. In all your ways acknowledge Him, and He will make your paths straight."*

It is hard to come away not realizing the scope of God's love for us focuses in on the smallest detail of our daily life.

Proverbs 16:9 also states:

> *"The mind of man plans his way,*
> *but the LORD directs his steps."*

These Scriptures in Proverbs have become life verses for me. As I look back over the "events" that brought me to where I am today, I cannot help but be in awe at the amazing trail of twists, turns, and surprises that undoubtedly have been infused with supernatural intervention and eternal purpose.

Now, back to my story. Goldendale was a small town with one main street and an intersection making it pretty easy to get around. As "circumstances" would have it, there was a Christian bookstore on the main corner one block from the garage where our vehicle had decided to stop running.

Walking into the bookstore was a breath of fresh air. There was the familiar feeling of family to this place—not to mention it was nice and toasty. The clerk asked if she could help us with anything so we proceeded to tell her the story of our current situation. She told us to hold on a minute and she picked up the phone and proceeded to make a phone call. Within a very short time our van was in the local garage being worked on and we found ourselves in a beautiful mountain home having dinner. "Good" news travels fast in a small town, and a local dentist heard about our dilemma and decided he would step in and help us out.

As the evening continued we explained that we were on our way back home to Tennessee for Christmas but it didn't look like we would make it now. The dentist's heart was moved and he decided to loan us a vehicle to make the trip home. Then after Christmas we would then drive back to Washington State to get our van. Needless to say we were very excited, the best part being that we didn't have to drive the fickle-fated UPS truck across the county. And as an added bonus, we would have heating that worked!

During the conversation the dentist made a comment that if we decided to stay in Goldendale, he would give us a house to live in and use as a home base so we could continue our ministry on the West Coast. We were surprised at the offer and said we would talk about it. After a few minutes of discussion everyone in the group thought it was a great idea. So we made the trip home for Christmas, turned around and drove back to Goldendale.

There is a town not too far away from Goldendale called Yakima. I discovered one day that Richard Probasco, the pastor of New Song Church in Portland, Oregon was going to be ministering at a church in Yakima called Shiloh Christian Center. I had wanted to see him for quite a while, so I decided to make the two-hour drive to Yakima.

Little did I know the biggest blessing of my life was about to take center stage. I was sitting toward the back of the church with some friends I had brought with me, from Goldendale, to the concert. When the service was over the very first person in the entire church to stand up was the most amazing girl I had ever seen in my life! She had been sitting on the front row in a dark blue business suit and when my eyes caught one glimpse of her I was undone. I decided I would move a little closer, so I walked right up to her and froze about ten feet away. Who was this gorgeous goddess with long brown hair I was staring at and why couldn't I get my feet to take another step? She proceeded to talk and greet people. Then before I knew it, she was gone. I got into my car and all I could do was think about her. The thought of her was burned into my heart.

The next day I told a very good friend of mine, Ken, about the concert and about this girl I had seen. As I began describing her, Ken stopped me in mid-sentence and said, "Oh, that's Cherrie (pronounced like Sheri). She is my fiancé's best friend." I just about fell over! The next words out of my mouth were, "Do you think your fiancé would give me her phone number?" He told me he was sure she would and within a few days I had Cherrie's number and was ready to give her a call.

Ken told me he was working at the mall in Yakima that weekend and was sure that Cherrie would stop by because his fiancé, Linda would be there. So I made plans to make that two-hour trip from Goldendale over Satus Pass to the mall in the Yakima Valley again, just for the chance that Cherrie might show up. I was so excited and nervous the night before that I was only able to sleep a few hours.

On my way to the mall, I started to get so nervous that I almost turned around and went home. I had no idea what to say to her, if she would even talk to me, or what to say if she did! What if she ignored me or didn't show up at the mall? I would have driven all that way for nothing.

I finally pulled into the parking lot and raced to the mall entrance only to be stopped by the huge knot in my stomach. I strolled around the other side of the mall pretending like I was shopping until I mustered up enough courage to go ahead and visit Ken. I couldn't wait any longer to see if he knew whether or not Cherrie was coming. But on my way inside I began to think, "What if she is already there? How can I just walk up and say hi?"

As I approached the store where Ken was working I noticed that he was alone. I felt a brief sense of relief as I went in and asked him if he knew if Cherrie would be there or not. He told me that she was supposed to show up but he didn't know when. I was a little disappointed because I had driven a long way and now it looked like it could take all day for me to meet her. I didn't know if I could handle the butterflies in my stomach increasing in number the longer I had to wait. As I looked down to the other end of the mall my stomach jumped into my throat. There she was. And she was walking straight in my direction!

I thought to myself, "Oh no! What do I say? How should I act?" But before I could make any sense of my mindless inhibitions, there she was, standing right in front of me.

I could feel the entire passage of time slow down as I looked at her and tried to catch my breath. "Hi," she said. "I'm Cherrie." Gulp! "Oh, hi. I'm Mike Kaylor," I replied back with my Southern accent. (Later on I found out she went home and told her mother that she had met a guy from Tennessee whose name is Mack Taylor!) Cherrie could only stay for a short time but those moments must have had six million seconds per minute in them. As she left I just stared, thinking, "There she goes: the tall, slender, bellbottom-jeans-wearing girl of my dreams."

It wasn't long after that I decided to call her. I only hung up a few times before I finally had the courage to let it ring long enough for her to answer. "Hello." "Hi, this is Mike. The guy you met at the mall, Ken's friend." She proceeded to tell me she was moving out of her apartment and back home with her parents. She thought it was kind of strange that the phone rang as it was in the process of being disconnected. With that introduction, I proceeded to ask if she would like to go with me to see a Christian band called Daniel Amos at a church in her town. She accepted, and to make a long story short, within six months we were married.

Are there divine "coincidences" that lead us into our destiny? Absolutely! I believe that if we will press into God for each area of our life, He will be faithful to direct our steps, no matter how unlikely they may seem.

I have great faith in the verse, "A man will plan his way but the Lord will direct his steps" (Proverbs 16:9, author's paraphrase). For me, a temporary tour to evangelize an area of the country through music turned into a lifetime of fulfilled purpose. The Lord is always faithful and always has our best interest at heart, as any good father would.

If you are searching for purpose and destiny in your life, ask yourself what that one thing is in your life you would love to be doing if money or time were not an issue? Many times, and I believe more often than not, much of our life's purpose is revealed in the deep unforgettable desires of our heart.

Many people have said to me, "I just want what Jesus wants." Have you ever thought that maybe He wants what you want and desire? Take a look at these verses:

John 16:24 says,

> *"Until now you have asked for nothing in My name; ask and you will receive, so that your joy may be made full."*

Whose joy is Jesus referring to? Your joy!

In Mark 11:24 (KJV) Jesus said,

> *"Ask whatever things you desire…"*

Who is supposed to ask? You are.

How about Psalm 37:4?

> *"So will your delight be in the LORD, and he will give you your heart's desires"* (author's paraphrase).

Whose heart's desires? Yours!

Some believers seem to be afraid to pursue their own dreams and desires because they don't want to seem arrogant, selfish, or "in the flesh." Let's be real: everyone in life has an agenda. Everyone does what they do for a desired outcome. Even those wishing to please God have a personal reason for what they do. It may be to satisfy a deep need of acceptance or a place of peace within them, knowing they have done something good. Or it may be out of simple devotion to someone they are passionate about. Whatever the reason, the truth is God favors you as His son and daughter, and as any good father, He wants to see your joy and desires in life be fulfilled.

It's okay to press into the areas of life you've always hoped for. It's good and right to pursue your God-given passions and dreams, even if they don't seem "spiritual," such as being a pastor or minister. The truth is we are all ministers[46] uniquely created to fulfill a destiny that can only be fulfilled by you. You are who you are because you where chosen from before time began to be in this time and season. I would say it's time to go for it. Why not? You have nothing to loose.

"Love God, and do what you wish."[47]

"Lord Jesus, I know that You have my life in the palm of Your hand. That You will never lead me from the path You have created me for. I ask that You make clear to me the area of my life that is uncertain. That You will show

[46] 2 Corinthians 5:18-20
[47] The Works of Saint Augustine: A New Translation for the 21st Century

me direction and confirmation on the decisions I make. I thank You that if it is important to me, I know it is also important to You. You know the very number of the hairs upon my head. Thank You that Your care for me is far greater than the care of the birds of the field. You will not let me down. You have never forsaken me. Once again I want to let You know how much I love You and need You and how grateful I am that You are in my life."

Chapter Twelve

I Don't Want to Die

Do not forget the benefits of the Lord,
...who heals all your diseases.
— Psalm 103:1-3 (author's paraphrase)

"We see, from almost every conceivable angle throughout the Scripture, that there is no doctrine more clearly taught than that it is God's will to heal all who have need of healing, and that they may fulfill the number of their days according to His promise."

- F. F. Bosworth

Two and a half years after getting married, Cherrie and I had a home, our own business, and a nine-month-old daughter named Stephanie. It was January and we where surrounded by snow and icy cold temperatures. My job as a carpenter often took me out into the bitter cold, but if I didn't work we had no income. The thermometer read five degrees as I headed out to frame the walls of the next home that I was building. Because of the extreme cold I could only work about half a day, but that was better than nothing. At least we would have some income coming in for that week.

After two weeks of working in these freezing winter conditions, I developed a cough. I didn't give much thought to it, thinking it was just a reaction to working in the cold temperatures. About a month later it became very obvious that something was wrong. The cough was worse, my appetite was gone, and I was losing weight rapidly. During the next two to three weeks I lost over twenty pounds.

I finally came to my senses and realized it might be a good idea to get checked out by a doctor. My wife had already been asking me to go to the doctor, so she was thrilled with my cooperation. It took a while to get an appointment, but when I finally got in the doctor immediately ordered X-rays. He was not sure about the cause of my condition, but said I should not have waited so long to get examined. About a week later I went back for my next appointment. The doctor told me that the X-rays showed my lungs were not clear. He began to explain to me that from the condition of my lungs I probably had one of three things. His hope was that I didn't have any of the three conditions, but if I did have one, it would not be the last thing on the list. Then he proceeded to tell me that I either had lung cancer, tuberculosis, or sarcoidosis. In order to determine which of the three I had, a biopsy was scheduled for the following week.

It would take two anxiety-filled weeks to get the biopsy results. During that time I looked at my wife and our new baby daughter and could not imagine leaving them. I did not want to die. How could I leave my wife without a husband and my daughter without a father? I was afraid.

It seems like we do our most concerted praying under times of distress. I was suddenly confronted with the possibility of death and it jolted me back to a vulnerable dependence on God. I knew if He did not show up, my life might soon be over. If I were going to get out of this it would have to be through the power of God.

Up until this point I knew of faith, but now I needed to know faith. It had to be alive in me. Because I had been mentored by a man of faith, Norvel Hayes, when I was younger, I knew one way to get the faith I needed during this time was to put the old cassette tapes of his teachings back into the player and listen to sermons about faith and healing from sun up to sun down. I had to get back to that place of radical faith I had once known. A place where the impossible situation I was facing would be confronted by the power of a far superior reality and overtaken with a demonstration of God's kingdom.

When the test results returned, the doctor called and asked if my wife and I would come to his office. The doctor sat behind his desk and began to tell me that if any good could come out from this test it was that I did not have cancer or tuberculosis. However, he paused for a moment before telling me that I did have sarcoidosis.

It was an incurable disease of unknown origin and the probability that it would continue to develop in my body was unquestionable. The disease would develop and spread in the organs and tissues of my body as a fatty substance, turning into scar-type tissue, which could eventually shut down the functionality of my organs, including my eyes. It was very possible that this disease would eventually be fatal. The doctor said that he wished he had better news. The only thing he could do for me was to prescribe Prednisone, a steroid, to help slow down the spread of the disease.

Looking into the eyes of my wife and daughter brought a determination that I was not going to lay down and die. I continued to feed myself on the nourishment of God's Word. The messages of healing and faith stirred my heart. I knew this disease was not from God and it was unquestionably God's heart to heal me. I found myself meditating on the Word like I had done years earlier. My words were words of expectation and I found myself trying to speak the way Jesus would speak in this situation. I knew words created an atmosphere and I needed the atmosphere of Heaven to surround me like never before.[48]

It would be three months before I would receive another full range of tests. During that time I continued to work and noticed that I was not getting as tired as I used to. I also noticed that my clothes were not falling off of me anymore. I anxiously awaited the return to the hospital because I knew something was different.

Three months passed and again they ran all of the tests. I went home and waited several days for a call from the doctor. When the call came, he asked if we could come since he wanted to talk to us in person. Not knowing exactly what was going on, I was a little nervous about the meeting.

When we arrived at his office, he placed a huge file containing all of my medical records on his desk. He then laid another file next to it with the results of the last barrage of tests I had taken. The doctor began by telling me I had unquestionably contracted sarcoidosis. The file sitting there was full of proof that the disease was rampant in my body. Then he said the new test results showed there was no trace of the disease in my body! He went on to tell us that he really didn't have any explanation for it and as far as he was concerned I had a clean bill of heath. The incurable disease was gone completely! I sat there with a smile on my face. That day we left his office, never to return.

---

[48] Proverbs 18:21

Meditating on the Word of God will bring life to your body and health to your soul.[49] Understanding that the promises of God are "Yes," as 2 Corinthians 1:20 (NIV) states: "For no matter how many promises God has made, they are 'Yes' in Christ." We can have confidence that the work of healing He begins in us will be completed. God substituted my physical condition of sickness for His wholeness and healing. Isaiah 53:4 says: "Surely our sicknesses He hath borne, and our pains—He hath carried them. And He is pierced for our transgressions, bruised for our iniquities, the chastisement of our peace is on Him, and by His bruise there is healing to us" (author's paraphrase).

As I focus my attention and my thoughts on the words of promise, I can come to a level of expectation that is rooted in the security of the unchanging Word of God. It becomes the foundation from which my life and my responses to situations are based.

Psalm 107:20 states:

> *"He sent His word and healed them, And delivered them from their destructions."*

In John 1:14 we know that Jesus is the living Word of God. Jesus came as the exact representation of the Father in the flesh to demonstrate the will and purposes of God.[50]

---

[49] Proverbs 4:20-23

[50] Hebrews 1:1-3

The will of God is healing—there is no que concerning this. God does not use sickness and disease to teach people lessons. Would any of you who have children place a disease like cancer on your child so that you could teach them a lesson? No. None of us would.

Read 1 John 3:8 (NIV):

> *"The reason the Son of God appeared*
> *was to destroy the devil's work."*

Jesus called the physical ailment that a woman had suffered under for eighteen years "a work of Satan" (Luke 13:18). Jesus equated sickness with the work of the enemy, not the work of God. Jesus always made the comparison of how much more your heavenly Father would do or be. If God did everything people accuse Him of doing, He would have to be arrested for child abuse.

In my prayer life, I constantly thank the Father in first person vernacular:

- "You carried my sickness and disease, and by Your stripes I am healed" - Isaiah 53.
- "You healed all who came to You" - Matthew 12:15.
- "You know what has happened throughout Judea, beginning in Galilee after the baptism that John preached—how God anointed Jesus of Nazareth with the Holy Spirit and power, and how He went around doing good and healing all who were

under the power of the devil, because God was with Him"– Acts 10:37-38.

- "You have sent Your word to heal me" – Psalm 107:20.
- "No weapon formed against me will prosper or succeed" – Isaiah 54:17.
- "Your will is that I prosper and be in health"– 3 John 1:2.
- "You have redeemed my life from the curse of sickness" – Galatians 3:13-14.
- "I remember Your benefits…Lord. You heal all of my diseases" – Psalm 103:1-3.
- "Your very name, Jehovah Rophe, is the God who heals me" – Exodus 15:26.

These are a few of the Scriptures that have become life to me. I pray them not because God needs to hear them, but because they increase my expectancy. You get what you expect. It's called Faith. Just as Jesus spoke the written Word of God to Satan[51] as a point of victory in the wilderness, so we speak the Word of God as a declaration of what He has already accomplished for us. It is not a prayer of incantation, but a prayer of expectation. The Word of God is alive. It is life to us. It brings us to a place where we simply believe God is going to do what He said He would do.

If you are dealing with a physical ailment, I encourage you to increase your intake of God's Word concerning

---

51 See Matthew 4:4, 7, 10; Deuteronomy 8:3; 6:13, 16. Jesus spoke the written Word of God, empowered with faith to defeat Satan's assault on Him.

healing. Begin to speak to the condition that is in your body and command it to leave. Jesus modeled this for us when He spoke to the fig tree and told it to become what He commanded.[52] Jesus also stood up on the bow of a boat and commanded a storm to cease.[53] He spoke to the body of a dead girl[54] as well as that of Lazarus:[55] both came back to life. Remember, Jesus said in John 20:21:

"As the Father has sent me, I also send you."

Speak life and healing back into your body!

Fill your heart with the encouraging truths of healing through works like F.F. Bosworth's Christ The Healer, and stories from books by John G. Lake and Smith Wigglesworth. Receive prayer from those who know the healing power of Jesus. Do yourself a favor and encourage yourself by hanging out with people who believe that with God all things are possible!

Let me pray for you now. "Father I spiritually lay my hands on any reader who is in need of healing. I bind all sickness and disease as it is bound in Heaven and release healing into their bodies now in Jesus' name. I loose divine health and newness of life. May all their days be days of health and lived to the fullness."

---

52 Mark 11
53 Mark 4:35-41
54 Mark 5:35-43
55 John 11:43-45

"Father I thank You that You are my healer—that every disease, germ, virus and bacteria that is afflicting me must die and leave my body in Jesus' name. Thank You that as You created me, You now recreate my body to return to normal and all the systems of my body would function in health. Body, I speak to you to receive your healing. Lord, as my hand extends to pray for others, Your hand extends. Thank You for stretching forth your Hand to heal!"

Chapter Thirteen

Encountered Destiny

I know the plans I have for you...
— Jeremiah 29:11

God's ways are a little unusual so you must stay in faith. He has a way to get you to your divine destiny.
Joel Osteen

My wife and I planted our first church in the 1980's. It was an adventure I will never forget. After several years of hard work, the church plant was finally coming into its own. We were looking at a new building for the church. We had come to a place where we were seeing the fruit of our labors.

One day, while driving home after taking my wife to work downtown, I began to have an experience that was totally new and quite unexpected. It's hard to find words to describe what was happening, except that it was like someone had jumped into my car unannounced.

Many of us would agree there is a feeling of familiarity we have when we are in our hometown. There is an emotional connection that lets us know we are home. As I was driving down the road, without any kind of notice, that emotional connection suddenly disappeared. I literally felt like I was a stranger driving in a strange town. Then a very odd thing happened. That emotional bond I had carried for years was replaced with a sense that my home was near the ocean. I thought to myself, "I don't live next to the beach."

The next thing that occurred was that an overwhelming presence filled my car. I had to focus to stay on the road. It was so strong; I knew I could not deny it was the presence of the Lord. As I began to think about what in the world was going on, it hit me. I grabbed the steering wheel with both hands and sternly said out loud,

"No! I am not moving!" After a few minutes I came to my senses and understood that the Lord may be calling us to move. I apologized to the Lord for being so stern and told Him I would be willing to relocate if He would take care of every detail. For the next few days, I was completely out of it. The effect of the presence of God brought me to a place of solemn quietness.

Soon after my encounter I had a dream. In the dream I was driving my car and the leader of the movement I was involved in at the time was sitting in the passenger seat. Suddenly I was driving on a map of the United States and was heading south. The dream appeared to confirm my experience in the car and at that point I knew we were going to be moving. Within four months we were packed. Our new church was close to the ocean and our new home was near the beach.

There is a scripture in the Old Testament that has become a life verse for me. The verse is found in Proverbs. In chapter 16 verse 9 it states:

"The mind of a man plans his way
but the Lord will direct his steps."

Supernatural directions may be a prerequisite to challenges that may be heading your way or they may be a way of rooting your destiny so the purpose of your life can be fulfilled. Either way we must let the Word of God have its perfect work in us during challenging times. Many people say that the storms and trials of life make us stronger. I couldn't disagree more. If trials and storms produced maturity then the earth would be filled with an army of mature believers destroying the works of the enemy in every country. But that is not the case.

It is not the trials that make us strong, but what we do in the middle of those trials. It is total abandonment and reliance on the Word of God that sustains us. It is faith and the application of His Word that matures us. Do we press into God during tough times or do we allow a wedge to be placed between God and us? Faith is the anchor for our soul. Faith is rooted in that which we cannot see.[56] Faith brings the unseen reality of what we need into the realm of this life. It is by faith that we live and move and have our being.[57]

If we encounter storms without a foundation of faith in His Word, we will be like a tree without roots or like a building with its foundation laid upon sand. We will be picked up and blown away by any type of pressure or circumstances that come our way.

If we allow faith, that confident endurance, to have its perfect work in us, we will be like a tree planted by the waters which produce fruit in due season. We can rest in the confidence that God is for us and He is on our side![58]

> "*Therefore everyone who hears these words of mine and puts them into practice is like a wise man who built his house on the rock. The rain came down, the streams rose, and*

[56] Hebrews 11:1
[57] Romans 10:8
[58] Romans 8:31; Psalm 27:1

> *the winds blew and beat against that house; yet it did not fall, because it had its foundation on the rock. But everyone who hears these words of mine and does not put them into practice is like a foolish man who built his house on sand. The rain came down, the streams rose, and the winds blew and beat against that house, and it fell with a great crash."*
>
> *Matthew 7-24-27*

For me, a deep sense of security comes from remembering the times in my past where God stood up for me when everything else seemed to be attacking me. Like David, who gained strength and courage by remembering how God had been with him to conquer the bear and the lion,[59] we too can move forward with the same assurance, knowing from past victories that He will never fail us or abandon us![60]

"Lord, I pray that the plans You have for me will continue to be revealed. That as I live my life, my destiny will unfold, and be fulfilled in the deepest way of experience. Lord, my love compels me to follow You, to know You. And I understand that to know You better, I must know Your presence and direction in my life. Thank You that even as I pray You are creating new adventures in my life that can only be accomplished if You are by my side. Once again I want to declare to You that I am in love with You."

[59] 1 Samuel 17:34-37
[60] Deuteronomy 31:6, 8

Chapter 14

The Lion's Roar

The lion has roared—who will not fear?
The Sovereign LORD has spoken—
Who can but prophesy?
— Amos 3:8

"A lion sleeps in the heart of every brave man."
Old Proverb

Getting together with other pastors in our church movement was always a great experience. The pastors meetings were a time when we could be together, strengthen the relational bonds, and just be ourselves.

One year we had the annual Pastors Retreat at a campground out in the middle of nowhere. I had no expectations except to hang out with everyone who was there. To be honest, I was sort of in a hurry for it to be over with. I had a backlog of things that needed to be done and I wanted to finish the projects that were looming over me.

It was during the time of worship in one of the morning meetings when I suddenly began to feel a strange sensation deep down inside of me. I knew from past experiences what this sensation was: it was the "river of living water"[61] building up like a geyser and was ready to explode. Immediately my mind recommended I should keep whatever was about to happen under control. I was well versed in the reasoning of my mind and knew God was up to something. It would be better to run with God than close the gate of my heart. So with no effort of choice I thought, "Let it come, Lord."

The presence kept building until I couldn't take it any longer. Within seconds I found myself bent over from a rush of energy flowing through my body, originating out

---

[61] John 7:38

of my innermost being. It kept coming like waves until I was down on the floor, on all fours. My mind was still trying to reason with me but there was no way I was going to let it stand in the way of this experiential flow of the tangible presence of God.

Suddenly, to my surprise and that of everyone else in the room, an extremely long, loud "roar" emerged from my mouth. Whether it was a loud voice, war cry, or a roar, it seemed like every cell of my body was crying out with intense sound and volume. It continued on and on until I collapsed, feeling totally emptied of strength but filled with an overwhelming sense that God was visiting me. While lying on my back, the sound continued until the tiny blood vessels on my forehead burst. Someone later made the comment that it looked like an artist had used a pencil and drawn a mane on my forehead.

After lying there for some time I got up and made my way to a chair. A few of the guys came over, but for the most part no one quite knew what to say. A friend of mine said he felt he had a word for me. He told me God had given me a coat of many colors like Joseph and that He intended for me to do all that He had gifted me in.

I had heard of people making sounds like a lion, but to be honest, I didn't quite know what to think about such events. Part of me thought that it could be God and another part thought it was just a fleshly response to the presence of the Holy Spirit. As I began to investigate my encounter, I came across a revival in Cane Ridge, Kentucky, in 1806 where people were accused of making sounds like animals and shaking until they fell to the ground. I thought to myself, "This is like reading a report of what happened to me that morning." The Lion of Judah always comes up when you begin to discuss this type of encounter. But I was looking for something in the Bible that would help the encounter make sense.

Then I found it: a text in Amos. When I read those words, I knew beyond a doubt I had experienced the Lord. Something in that Scripture leapt out and grabbed my heart. I do not believe it is a coincidence that the verse concerning the roar of a lion is placed between two Scriptures on prophecy. The lion's roar is a declaration of sovereignty of the prophetic voice of the Lord.

In fact, Amos begins his prophetic message by writing, "The LORD roars from Zion" (Amos 1:2, NIV). Here is what follows in Amos 3:7-8 (NIV):

> "Surely the Sovereign LORD does nothing without revealing his plan to his servants the prophets.
>
> The lion has roared—who will not fear? The Sovereign LORD has spoken—who can but prophesy?"

Have I noticed an increase of the prophetic ministry in my life after this encounter? Yes. Did I need the encounter to prophesy? No. It was a sign to me that my loving Father wanted to pour more of who He was into my life.

I know a lot of people criticize the sounds that have been heard in renewal meetings. As I mentioned before, I didn't give much credence to them myself until I had this experience. There is something about an experience that transforms your view of reality as well as theology. I've learned that to ignore something because it doesn't fit into my worldview will limit my ability to understand the expanse of God. I have come to understand the manifestations from God are meant to bring transformation, not just exhilaration.

If God will shake an entire building or a mountain to make a declaration,[62] then is it a small thing to produce the roar of a lion to prophetically declare His authority, courage, and victory over the life of His son or daughter?

Let me give you another example—another testimony.

A few years ago on a ministry trip in Brazil, a team of leaders from a wonderful church named The Garden in Bakersfield, California, asked for an appointment for ministry and impartation with Cherrie and myself. That afternoon we prayed for a man who was quiet and reserved, but hungry for all God had for him. As I was praying I began to hear the sound of the roar of a lion over his house. The Lord also told me to call him "Richard the Lionhearted." I turned and asked one of the members on his team what his name was. She said it was Rick. As I continued to pray for Rick, I began to prophetically declare, "You are Richard the Lionhearted!" I spoke this over him three times. On the third time Rick began to roar with such volume that the people outside the building, swimming underwater in the pool, heard it and came running to see what was happening. Rick continued to

---

[62] See Acts 4:31 and Exodus 19:18.

roar until he was exhausted and laying on the floor of the conference room. We all participated in the joy that this man had just encountered the Lion of Judah.

About a year later we were speaking at The Garden Church in Bakersfield, California, where Rick is a leader. When I asked him if he had noticed a difference before and after the "roaring" event he told me he felt more boldness and authority than he ever had before this experience.

I believe the Holy Spirit activated something in Rick's life that would enable him to move forward in his destiny. It was manifestation for transformation. For all of us, it was an amazing experience.

One other thought I want you to consider: remember that it was after the roaring or groaning that I received the prophetic word from my friend concerning the coat of many colors. What if I had quenched the Spirit that day and put being "respectable" above my desire to move with God? I believe yielding to this experience stirred up prophetic declarations and released destiny.

My friend Gary Oates described in his book, Open My Eyes Lord, a similar point of decision. During worship, Gary felt the quiet impression to take off his shoes because he was standing on holy ground. In his mind he resisted because the floor was dirty. But in simple obedience, he removed his shoes. He believes today that if he had said no to the removal of his shoes—if he had not yielded to the "quiet roar"—he would not have experienced what followed. A few moments after he removed his shoes,

Gary's eyes were opened and he began to see into the heavenly realm. He has never been the same since that simple act of yielding to the voice of God.

Jonathan Edwards, the great revivalist of the 18th Century, comments on this type of encounter with these words:

> *"It was very wonderful to see how person's affections were sometimes moved, when God did as it were suddenly open their eyes, and let into their minds a sense of the greatness of His grace, the fullness of Christ, and His readiness to save...Their joyful surprise has caused their hearts as it were to leap, so that they have been ready to break forth into laughter, tears often at the same time issuing like a flood, and intermingling a loud weeping. Sometimes they have not been able to forebear crying out with a loud voice, expressing their great admiration. The manner of God's work on the soul, sometimes especially, is very mysterious."*[63]

I encourage you to yield to God's simple impressions and watch how God will use your act of faith to activate a deeper encounter with Him. Give yourself permission to believe that even greater experiences than these are yours!

"Lord, I am ready for more. I need more of You and do not care how it looks or what it feels like. I am hungrier for You than the approval of my friends. I care more about

---

[63] A Faithful Narrative of the Surprising Work of God by Jonathan Edwards

what You think than what all of the other people think about me. So I invite You and the Holy Spirit to come to me. I need You more than the air I breathe. Help me experientially understand that with You there is no end to the 'more.' Set me up and then encounter me! Your divine encounters with me are what I want. I give You permission to come upon me and into my life greater than I can think or imagine."

Chapter Fifteen

The Sign That Made Us Wonder

God can do anything, you know—
far more than you could ever imagine
or guess or request in your wildest dreams!
— Ephesians 3:20 (The Message)

"There is never an end
to the 'more' of God."
– Michael Kaylor

Usually when "signs in the heavens" are mentioned, it is a reference to the second coming of Christ. In this case it is a reference to a remarkable event that still leaves me speechless.

I had been ministering in Brazil for over three weeks and was looking forward to returning home for a rest. My wife Cherrie and daughter Tiffany were also on the trip with me. Our last week in Brazil, we were in a town on the eastern coast called Maceió. It was a beautiful town with palm trees along the coast and waves that washed over the beach in a rhythmical motion that could easily lull you into a restful daydream.

During our stay we met a man who was known as a prophet and pastor in the area. The man, Pastor Helio, was very unassuming and a quiet type—that was until he got behind the pulpit. Then he was on fire. He preached with passion that left everyone knowing his message was truly from God. His love for God was evident.

Our first meeting with him was at his church after a midweek service. We sat and waited while he talked with some of his parishioners at the end of the service. What I overheard was pretty amazing. Pastor Helio was speaking things that were unknowable except to the people themselves and to God. After everyone had left, he sat down with us and began to call out things in our life he had no way of knowing. We were amazed. I have seen this type of prophetic ministry before, but seldom this level of accuracy. After being ministered to concerning things of our family and church, we left with a fresh awareness of the awesomeness of God and His heart to interact with us.

Over the next few days we met with him three different times. It was more of a relationship building time, but he seemed to live with his gift operating at all times. Here is an example. The day before we met with Pastor Helio there was a comical event that happened during our drive through the city. Our friend and translator were joking around with our daughter about the type of guy she should marry. Of course we all laughed when she, in no uncertain terms, told him that he was wrong, then proceeded to describe the type of person she would choose. A day later, as we sat with the pastor, he suddenly began to repeat the event exactly as if he'd been in the car, including a confirmation of Tiffany's choice of a future husband. We all broke out in laughter, but the laughter was partly a response to the shock of his insight.

Later on that day the pastor said he would like to bless us and asked if we would go to the beach with him that evening. Of course we all said yes, wondering what Pastor Helio had for us.

That night we all piled into a small Brazilian car and headed up the road to a secluded beach on the coast. The dirt road to the beach had the deepest potholes I have ever seen. In fact, I concluded that if we were to ever hit one, we'd never get out. To avoid such pitfalls, we drove with the precision of a fine stunt driver.

As we finally pulled onto the beach itself, a sigh of relief erupted from everyone in the car. We'd made it. (Of course this little excursion pales in comparison to another trip we had just made in which a rioting crowd of machete-waving, hostile people attacked our car).

We all rolled out of the car and stretched our arms. It was an amazingly clear night filled with a breeze that felt like a fresh breath from Heaven. Pastor Helio was excited and motioned for us all to follow him onto the sand by the ocean. The waves were rolling in, illuminated by the bright moon and the diamond-studded sky.

Pastor Helio grabbed my hand, and through our translator, Paulo, said he was going to ask God to give me a sign that my ministry would be known around the world. I was a little taken back and just said, "Okay." I wasn't quite sure what to think about his statement, but I was anxious to see what he was going to do next. He pointed to one particularly beautiful, colored star. The star was amazing—a flickering jewel of blue and green. Pastor Helio instructed us to gaze at the star as he prayed. Then he fell to his knees and lifted his hands and voice to the Lord.

After a few minutes of watching the star, I wondered what he was praying for, since his fervency and passion were increasing very loudly in Portuguese. We watched the star as it continued to blink its multi-colors, seeming to grow brighter and brighter. Then suddenly, without any forewarning, the star that we all had been watching vanishing into thin air! It was gone! Our jaws dropped, standing speechless on this amazing beach. Pastor Helio jumped up and down with great excitement. He ran to us and began to hug each of us with laughter and joy like someone who had just received an amazing gift at Christmas.

What in the world do you do with something like that? A star vanished right before our eyes! I looked at Tiffany and Cherrie, they looked back at me, and we just stood there, frozen in time. How do you process something like that? In reality, that star was a sun. Now it was gone. Did it cease to exist or was it an inexplicable event that was to be treasured only at this time and in this part of the galaxy?

No matter what the answer, one thing is for sure: it was an event I will forever remember. It marked an opening of a new dimension of God's grace and love in our lives. Even the stars would be a gift to demonstrate His amazing love for us.

Since that experience I have learned the valuable lesson of not taking lightly the works of the Lord. That one event has been a tool in God's hand, helping me to stand when it seemed like nothing would work and everything was falling apart. My remembrance of that night has enabled me to continue on and stay the course when nothing around me made any sense. It brought me to a place where faith has a new dimension.

No matter how small or how extreme a sign from God may be, we must by all means consider the source and know that a God who can hang the sun and the stars in the sky can easily create an open door for His purpose and destiny in our lives.

The more we look, the more we will find. The more we knock, the more doors will be opened. None of us can afford to become stagnant or get stuck in a routine in our life with Him.

If you are hungry, there is always more. It may come at a time when you least expect it or want it, but it will come. The cry for more is always answered. When we look at our life we can see times of God's supernatural intrusion to answer our longing for a life beyond the realm of the mundane.

I encourage you to review your life and ask Him to show and illuminate the encounters of the past that may have gotten overlooked or ignored. He will begin to build a story of your life in which the One who was always with you, will always be with you. The One who breathed life in you will once again become the air that saturates every fiber of your being. Just ask Him. He is faithful.

My prayer is that God would give us more than we are asking for! Let Your extravagant abundance overtake us.

Let Your Kingdom come…

"Look at the stars, Abraham
—And believe I Am."[64]

I pray your life's journey will expose the hand of God in a dimension that will transform your life and annihilate any hindrances you may be carrying. I also pray that you would begin to live from Heaven toward earth knowing that His great power has granted to you those things that are beyond what you can think or imagine. I pray His experiential love and interaction will become a precious and valuable treasure. I pray your life is forever changed as you gaze upon Him. And may the breath of His voice refresh you in ways you had only dreamed of in the past. Let each day from this day forward become a day of new beginnings as you launch out on the adventure of supernatural discovery.

64 "Abraham" Phil Keaggy - Love Broke Through 1976

For more information of other teaching resources from Mike and Cherrie you can contact them at:

Kaylor Ministries
PO Box 770488
Coral Springs, FL 33077
or email at
contact@kaylorministries.com

"When The Fire Falls"

This CD is the testimony of Mike's encounters with God. As you listen, your heart will open for more of Him and the prayer for impartation will encourage and encounter your life. You may never be the same again.

"Releasing Heaven Through Intercession"

This is a two part CD set in which Cherrie Kaylor explains levels of intercession and then on the second CD, prays with you concerning healing. The entire second CD is praying healing scriptures. If you are in need of healing or have someone that needs healing then you may want to consider this set. The testimonies that have come back have been amazing.

"Restored To Royalty"

This set will bring you into a place of wholeness and freedom and help erase the effects of you past. Sometimes the patterns repeat and we feel like we are going around the mountain again. God has an amazing destiny for you. Letting go of the past will free us to move forward into our divine destiny.

"Discover A Life Of Increase"

This two-part CD unlocks the truth of supernatural provision. The heart of God is that He wants you to have more than enough in life. The set helps re-adjust our belief system to agree with God's heart and the steps for releasing impartation upon your finances.

To view other resources or to order visit:
www.kaylorministries.com